Hitler's Early Raiders

Hitler's Early Raiders

Robert McQueen

Whittles Publishing

Published by
Whittles Publishing Ltd.,
Dunbeath,
Caithness, KW6 6EG,
Scotland, UK

www.whittlespublishing.com

© 2011 Robert McQueen

ISBN 978-1904445-852

Printed by Bell & Bain Ltd., Glasgow

Contents

Preface

The first air raids on Britain were, to put it mildly, unimpressive. In many ways it seemed an odd sort of war. Waves of Nazi bombers darkening the sky and raining death on fearful civilians could not have been further from the truth.

The early attacks on the British coastline during the so-called 'Phoney War' period, were, for the most part, little more than reconnaissance 'feelers' aimed at locating and testing the British coastal defences.

A lone Nazi aircraft was intercepted and forced down by R.A.F fighters within weeks of the outbreak of war, on 26 October 1939, close to the village of Humbie in the Lammermuir hills, ten miles from Edinburgh. The 'Humbie Heinkel', as it was later known, was the first enemy aircraft to be brought down over Britain.

As a young schoolboy growing up in post-war Edinburgh, I was fascinated by a photograph of the 'Humbie Heinkel' I found in my local library. Many young boys of my generation were weaned on flying adventure stories, like Biggles, or wartime heroes such as Guy Gibson of Dam Buster fame.

Years later as a young journalist I decided to research the early war. The Heinkel was to become a pivotal part of my book research!

Hitler had decreed that attacks on shipping were permitted, but only as long as they were on the High Seas. Not a single civilian was to be killed, as Berlin still hoped to obtain a quick settlement of the conflict with Great Britain.

In 1919, the Treaty of Versailles decreed that Germany should have its navy placed under severe restrictions. The surface fleet was limited to six heavy and six light cruisers and 24 torpedo boats. In 1929, Admiral Raeder had become Commander in Chief (Grossadmiral) of the Navy. He wanted to build a new, balanced fleet as soon as he could.

One important development began in 1928, because the German naval staff had spotted a loophole in the Versailles Treaty and the Washington Naval Treaty of 1922. This allowed them to build the so-called 'pocket battleships'. The first – *The Deutschland* – was launched in 1929. These pocket battleships were specifically designed with surface raiders in mind. They had two turrets and three 11-inch guns, carried fore and aft, and could sail at a top speed of 28 knots. They were capable of a maximum range of over 2,100 miles before refuelling. They were only 600 feet in length and displaced only between ten and 12 thousand tons. They were extremely formidable, fast and equipped to deliver lethal fire power.

These raiders shared the problems, and some of the methods, of pirates in the 17th and early 18th centuries. They used disguises to approach their prey, displaying false flags in a very similar fashion. They opened fire on their unsuspecting enemies at the last possible moment, and used intimidation to force a quick surrender.

Despite the precautions of the German naval staff in appearing to adhere to the Hague Convention, the unescorted passenger liner, S.S. *Athenia* was torpedoed with the loss of 100 passengers, late on the evening of 3 September 1939. The sinking of the vessel some 200 miles due west of the Hebrides, whilst en route to Montreal from Liverpool, signalled the start of hostilities at sea.

Lieutenant Lemp, the submarine commander admitted responsibility for the sinking but maintained he had been over-excited by Britain's sudden declaration of war.

Special thanks to:

R. Behnisch
A. Imrie
J. Kerr
G. Pinkerton
H. Pohle
H. Vogel
J. Ward

Every effort has been made to render as accurate a story as possible, but the author apologises for any omissions or inaccuracies that may remain.

S.S. *Anglo Saxon* crew list

August 1940

Article Order

Name	Capacity	POB	Last Ship	Age
FLYNN, Philip R L	Master	Plymouth	Same	53
DENNY, Barry C	Mate	London	Same	31
DUNCAN, Alistair St. C	2nd Mate	Stromness	Same	28
PICKFORD, Walter M	3rd Mate	Wallasey	*Shivan*	30
O'LEARY, Michael	1 R/Offr	Killarney	Same	48
PILCHER, Roy H	2 R/Offr	Durham	Same	21
HANSEN, Oscar W	Carpenter	Denmark	*Sandsend*	47
MAHER, Thomas F	Bosun	Duncannon	Same	34
ELLIOTT, Stanley G	A.B.	Nantyglo	*Marquesa*	22
WIDDICOMBE, Roy W C	Sailor	Totnes	*Quebec City*	21
BRESLER, Adolphus	A.B.	Russia	*British Zeal*	45
SMITH, Alfred E	Sailor	Grimsby	*Rushpool*	41
SAVORY, Robert	Sailor	Grimsby	*Amberleigh*	33
ALLNATT, Walter R T L	A.B.	Fleetwood	*Leeds City*	28
GORMLEY, James J	Sailor	Monaghan	*Hopestar*	24
PROWSE, William F	O.S.	Newport	*Anacataca*	18
TAKLE, Philip J	O.S.	Cardiff	*Masimda*	16
PENNY, Francis G	Gunner	Mortimer	Same	44
TAPSCOTT, Robert G	A.B.	Bristol	*Orford*	19
MILBURN, Edward E	Ch. Engr	North Shields	Same	39
HOUSTON, John I	2nd Engr	Lisburn	Same	55
HAWKS, Lionel H	3rd Engr	Dublin	*Columbia Star*	23
RICE, Thomas A	4th Engr	South Shields	First ship	20
NICHOLAS, Alfred J	Donkeyman	Plymouth	Same	37
FOWLER, James	Greaser	Newport	*City of Cairo*	37
WILLIAMS, Charles H	Greaser	Barry	Same	29
WILLIAMS, David J	F/Trimmer	Barry	Same	20
GREEN, Verdun C	F/Trimmer	Barry	Same	24
ELEY, Albert	F/Trimmer	Swansea	*Lurigethan*	26
TENOW, Frederick	F/Trimmer	Estonia	*John Holt*	58
RASMUSSEN, Lars C	F/Trimmer	Denmark	*Peterton*	53

STUART, Charles	F/Trimmer	Newport	*Sulaoo*	44
PEASTON, John D	F/Trimmer	West Ham	Same	29
WALLACE, Charles J	F/Trimmer	Newport	*Fowberry Tower*	21
WARD, George W	Asst Stwd	South Shields	Same	19
BEDFORD, George	Cook	Newport	*Peterton*	21
MORGAN, Leslie J	Asst Cook	Newport	*Robert L Holt*	20
KEYSE, Trevor	M/R Stwd	Newport	*Mill Hill*	19
OLIVER, Andreas	F/Trimmer			26
TOBIN, H.	F/Trimmer			35
WILLIS, Harry A	Ch. Stwd Newport			40

C.H. Williams and D.J Williams were brothers.

Failed to join

STANTON, F	A.B	Newport	*Glentilt*	23
WALSH, John	Greaser	Manchester	First ship	29
DAVIS, J (?)	F/Trimmer	Liverpool	*Tetela*	40
WHITEHORN, RH	Ch. Stwd	Winchester	Same	56

Tapscott replaced Stanton, Oliver and Tobin replaced Walsh and Davis, Willis replaced Whitehorn, only Tapscott signed the main articles.
Whitehorn was later lost on *Anglo Peruvian* 23 February 1941.

Raider 'D' Cruise
SCHIFF 21 HSK 3 *WIDDER*
ROUTE 6.5.40–31.10.40

6.5.40	Depart Kiel
21.5.40	Entered North Atlantic
13.6.40	Tanker *British Petrel*, heading for Trinidad in ballast, sunk.
26.6.40	Norwegian tanker *Krossfonn*. Taken as prize and sent to Lorient. She was bound from Fort de France from Casablanca. No cargo – in ballast.
10.7.40	*Davisian* sunk. She was bound from Cardiff to Trinidad and Barbados. No cargo – In ballast.
13.7.40	*King John* sunk. In ballast – bound from Vancouver to London.
4.8.40	Norwegian tanker *Beaulieu*. Bound from Aruba to Azores.
8.8.40	Dutch vessel *Oostplein* sunk. Bound Buenos Aires from Cardiff and Hull with coal.
10.8.40	Finnish barque *Killoran* sunk. Laden with maize and sugar, bound Las Palmas from Buenos Aires.
21.8.40	*Anglo Saxon* sunk. Bound from Bahia Blanca from Newport with coal. Sunk at Lat. 26.10 N, Long. 34.09 W.
2. 9.40	Tanker *Cymbeline* sunk. Bound for Trinidad in ballast.

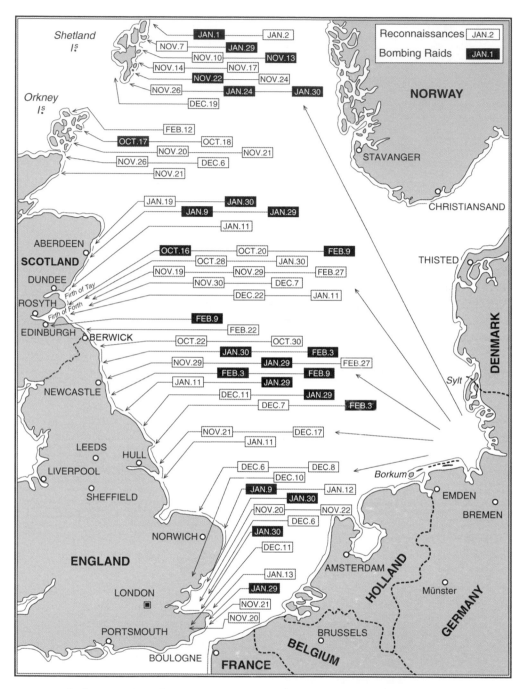

The first Nazi air raid on Britain occurred on October 16, 1939. Between that date and February 27 there were 74 reconnaissance and bombing raids on our shores. This chart shows the part of our coast reached on each occasion by the German planes. The distances travelled by the raiding plane, out and home, range from 400 miles (to the Norfolk coast) to over 1,000 miles (to the Shetlands). It is estimated that at least 38 of the planes employed on the raids were destroyed by our fighters, and that the raids thus cost Hitler £1,000,000.

1 · Unreal conflict

The first Luftwaffe raids on Britain were hardly impressive during those early days of the 'Phoney War' between 3 September 1939 and 9 May 1940. In many ways it seemed an odd sort of war. For a number of years some leading observers had forecast swarms of Luftwaffe bombers filling up the sky and raining death and destruction on a terrified populace. Apart from two major attacks on 9 October and 16 October against elements of the Home Fleet, most of the early raiders made their appearance in ones and twos, and enemy bombs were mainly discharged on strictly military, or rather, naval targets. The bulk of the aerial activity consisted of exploratory raids, mine-laying and reconnaissance sorties.

Fresh from their successes in Poland, the battle-hardened crews of the crack Luftwaffe squadrons had been issued with strict orders not to drop bombs on the country of the antagonist. Hitler had decreed that attacks on shipping were permitted but only as long as they were on the High Seas. Not a single civilian was to be killed as Berlin still hoped to obtain a quick settlement of the conflict with Great Britain. Military necessities at that stage of the war were to be subordinated to political considerations.

Mistakes by both Britain and Germany were, of course, inevitable during the tense early days of this unreal conflict. Early in September 1939 an RAF raider dropped a bomb over the port of Esbjerg, Denmark and killed two persons. A few days later three RAF bombers flew over Belgium and, when a Belgian plane signalled them to land, shot it down. A week later, near Warsaw, German planes unloaded six bombs on the villa of the US Ambassador, A. J. Drexel Biddle, jun., who claimed that the raid was deliberate. The first British civilian was killed on 16 March 1940, during a German raid at Hatston in the Orkney Islands.

Following Hitler's march into Czechoslovakia, which was aimed at outflanking Poland, he began to press for the return of the German part of Poland.

At the beginning of June 1939 the Home Fleet sailed into Weymouth for a review. By the end of August 1939 the ships were gathering at Scapa Flow under war orders although war had still not broken out. The arrival of the Royal Naval Hospital Ship *St Abba*, painted white with red crosses, was an ominous sign to the sailors. Defences were poor at Scapa and obviously did not take into account the aerial photography employed by the Germans. Warships were at great risk from an air attack, lying in an underdefended base.

The Luftwaffe was thought capable of an 800-bomber attack on Scapa Flow, a ratio of 100 bombers to every heavy AA gun there. The Commander in Chief of the Home Fleet, Admiral

Forbes, heard this startling news on 7 September. All leading units of the Home Fleet had been moved from one anchorage to another in the hope of evading attack. The main threat was considered to be from the air. The 29,000 ton battleship *Royal Oak* was anchored in the remote north-east corner of the Flow, where her AA guns could protect her from air attack.

Ironically, the first real successes against the British were achieved by the U-boats. On 17 September *U-29*, under Lieutenant Commander Schuhard, had sunk the British aircraft carrier *Courageous*, west of Ireland. And in the early hours of 14 October Lieutenant Commander Prien, with *U-47*, made a daring entry into the Flow to achieve only partial success. The British Fleet, presumed to be in anchorage there, had already put out to sea. Prien promptly dealt with *Royal Oak*, holing her with two salvoes of three torpedoes each, before she sank with the loss of 833 officers and men. Prien's audacious exploit led, two days later, to an action by Ju 88 dive bombers. German air reconnaissance units were now continually shadowing the passage of ships on the Scottish east coast.

There had been a tendency to overestimate the strength of the Luftwaffe. Churchill had once referred to Germany's 20,000 first-line aircraft, which had caused the aeronautical press in Britain to regard this as a joke. In September 1939 the Luftwaffe numbered about 4,500 first-line aircraft and the German aircraft industry was producing 700 planes a month but had the capability of producing double. The Heinkel He III, a medium bomber, was built at Heinkel's Orienburg factory and delivered on 22 August 1939 as III EN of 5/KG 26 based at Westerland, on the Frisian island of Sylt.

As early as 1936 a squadron for 'special purposes' had been subordinated to the General Staff of the Luftwaffe's 5th Branch (intelligence). Goering obtained top personnel, aircraft and equipment. Pilots were recruited who had the necessary background knowledge. Most of them had worked for aerial photography firms, international commercial carriers and aircraft manufacturers. Air adventurers such as Count Hoensbroech and Count Saurma joined the squadron. The camera-manufacturing company Carl Zeiss had developed advanced aerial cameras which were later used effectively by the Luftwaffe during the war. The squadron's first functional aircraft was the new twin-engine low-wing monoplane developed by Ernst Heinkel in the mid-1930s as the fastest passenger plane in the world, and as a speedy medium bomber. This was the He III, capable of carrying a four-man crew to a normal range of 2,000 miles. Its great quality was its stability in the air (due to its great weight), which made it ideal for aerial photography.

In the late 1930s the squadron flew missions against Britain, Poland, France, Russia and Czechoslovakia. Although most of the 'spy' missions started from Germany, some planes were stationed in Budapest. Flying from the Hungarian capital posed no problems as the Hungarians were considered to be friendly. Sites in south-eastern Europe were easily accessible from Budapest. The squadron was acting under instructions from Josef 'Beppo' Schmid, head of Luftwaffe Intelligence. Many missions provided photographs of potential bomb targets, while some photographs were of strategic importance only, such as armaments factories. Other missions were operational, such as those to photograph border fortifications and interior road networks. Some of the pilots even pretended to be testing out new airline routes. From Stavanger, in southern Norway, German aircraft could reach Scapa Flow in less than forty minutes.

Each reconnaissance unit had a photographic section situated at the airfield. The darkrooms, evaluation areas and reproduction sections were housed in half a dozen trucks to make the section as mobile as the air unit itself, and it moved from airfield to airfield as the force advanced or retreated. The photo section was self-contained with its own hundred-gallon water supply, light tables, enlargers, celluloid triangles, graduated steel rules, loupes, magnifying glasses, slide rules and coloured pencils.

During the war Germany built some 6,299 reconnaissance aircraft, which represented 5.5 per cent of its total production of 113,515 aircraft. At the outbreak of war, the Luftwaffe had 260 long-range reconnaissance aircraft. In the early days of the war the Luftwaffe's chief long-range reconnaissance plane was the Dornier Do 17F, an adaptation of a medium bomber originally designed in about 1935. It was a long-fuselage twin-engine, twin-tail machine, with pilot, observer/cameraman, radioman/gunner, but had a very low service ceiling of 18,000 feet. Two such machines, which proved to be easy prey for RAF fighters, were shot down over southern England in late November 1939.

One of the most prominent squadrons to take part in early raids over the British coastline was the Kampfgeschwader (KG) 26 unit, which mainly operated from its base at Lübeck–Blankensee. The squadron had received the name of 'Lion Squadron' from its first commander, later to be Generalfeldmarschall Freiherr von Richthofen.

Operating from bases in France, Denmark, Norway and northern Germany Kampfgeschwader 26 with its special crews attacked important targets on the coastal regions of Britain. All of the squadron's aircraft took part in the 9 October raid and a Heinkel He III of KG 26 crash-landed on a Scottish hillside on 28 October, the first enemy aircraft to be brought down intact on the British mainland during the Second World War.

The Germans were strong, but only in comparison to British weaknesses. In reality the Luftwaffe, by sacrificing bomb-loads for fuel, was capable of attacking with 400 bombers. Scapa had eight heavy AA guns but there were no short-range AA guns and no high-performance fighters.

As the last shots of the Polish campaign died away, Hitler turned his attention to the main enemy, the British Fleet. He was unable to match it at sea and in a direct action because his main interests were focused on the East, which prevented him from building an adequate number of ships. He was weak, even in submarines, but as the former High Seas Fleet had been scuttled in Scapa Flow during the First World War, those he did have were mostly new, whereas what the Royal Navy had were mostly old.

A carefully planned campaign including warships, submarines, mines and aircraft could all contribute to him eliminating, within a few months, a sizeable proportion of the British Home Fleet. After that, his armies would then be able to gain forward bases in Holland, Belgium and northern France. From such bases he would then be able to wage war on British sea communications, resulting, if successful, in a peace settlement with Britain and France. This would enable him to be free for his assault on Russia.

On 6 September 1939 the first German reconnaissance flight over Scapa was made by a weather aircraft of Luftflotte 2 (Air Fleet 2) and a day later the Admiralty warned Admiral Forbes that with the Home Fleet at Scapa an attack by 800 bombers was possible. A photograph taken on 6 September which showed both the main fleet anchorage and destroyer anchorage, with ships in them, reached the desk of Kommodore Doenitz, commanding the U-boat arm on 11 September. Doenitz wanted more information and on the 13th sent out *U-14* to patrol the Orkneys and report on the coast defences and the currents. When it returned on the 29th its captain said he thought a U-boat could penetrate Hoxa Sound when the gate was opened. More reconnaissance aircraft flew over Scapa, so high that the sound of their engines could not be heard, out of range of the AA guns and the reach of British naval fighters.

The British Government had purchased from the Marquis of Linlithgow in 1903 the shorelines surrounding Rosyth Castle, which was built in 1560, and constructed a base which became one of the largest in the world, capable of docking and repairing all classes of war vessels and minor craft making use of Port Edgar on the South Shore. The Firth of Forth, with a succession of powerful batteries along both sides and on the islands, was generally considered impregnable, and the strategic value of the base was fully proved in both world wars. The first German air attack on British territory took place against warships in the Firth of Forth on 16 October. Two cruisers and a destroyer were damaged and two Ju 88s were shot down by Spitfires, the first victories by Britain-based fighters.

Fundamental lessons about the vulnerability of unescorted bombers in daylight were learnt during December 1939 in three attacks made on the Heligoland area by a formation of RAF Wellingtons. On the second occasion five of the twelve aircraft were shot down, and on the 18th, when 24 bombers were unable to find German shipping due to cloud, BF 109s and BF 110s attacked and shot down twelve of them; three more made forced landings on return.

Throughout this period both sides had refrained from making bombing attacks on each other's territory, though British and French bombers had flown many night sorties over Germany only to drop propaganda leaflets.

However, as a result of the first German bombs falling on British soil during the Hatston raid, Bomber Command Whitleys raided Hornum seaplane base on Sylt the next night. The French, however, requested that no further such attacks be made for fear of escalation in the air war with the Luftwaffe.

The RAF's first raid of the war took place on 4 September, when Blenheim and Wellington bombers raided Wilhelmshaven naval base. Five Blenheims and two Wellingtons were shot down, the Wellingtons claimed by Feldwebel Aldred Held was the first Luftwaffe victory in the West. Damage to German warships was only slight. The RAF, restricted like the Germans to purely maritime targets, began daylight operations in force across the North Sea late in September.

The Chief of Staff's review of the defence of Scapa Flow after the declaration of war had made it clear that many interests and many pressures were involved in maintaining the security of the Fleet. The War Office had to provide the guns but could not consider weakening Britain's air defence programme, which consumed all the 3.7 inch artillery available. Despite the recommendations that two fighter squadrons, which could, in an emergency, be reinforced by five more, should be made available, it was felt that the air defence of Britain, still short of 15 squadrons, would be further depleted by moving two to Scapa Flow.

The attack on Scapa Flow and loss of the *Royal Oak* provoked instant reactions in the Admiralty. On 31 October, accompanied by the First Sea Lord, Churchill went to Scapa Flow to hold a second conference on these matters in Admiral Forbes's flagship. Against air attack it was planned to mount 88 heavy and 40 light AA guns together with numerous searchlights and increased barrage-balloon defences. Substantial fighter protection was to be maintained both at Orkney and at Wick on the mainland. It was hoped that all the arrangements could be completed to enable the Fleet to return by March 1940.

Possible alternative bases were considered. Admiralty opinion favoured the Clyde, but Admiral Forbes felt that the distance factor was too great. The other alternative was Rosyth, which had been Britain's main base towards the end of the First World War. Although its location was considered suitable, it was thought to be vulnerable to air attack.

During the first month's raids, the RAF fighters proved themselves more than a match for the enemy machines. Equally, the ground and naval anti-aircraft defences, equipped with ultra-modern detecting and gun-laying equipment, provided a deadly barrage against enemy air activity.

The early raids, with the possible exception of the Firth of Forth attacks, were, for the most part, little more than reconnaissance 'feelers' aimed at locating and testing the British coastal defences.

2   Raeder's balanced fleet

Before beginning to look at the detail of the German naval activities in the early part of the war, it is worthwhile to look at the political background to the whole conflict.

By the Treaty of Versailles Germany had had its navy placed under very severe restrictions. The surface fleet was limited to six heavy and six light cruisers and 24 torpedo boats. In 1929 Admiral Raeder had become Commander in Chief (Grossadmiral) of the German navy. He wanted to build a new, balanced fleet as soon as he could.

One very important development began in 1928, because the German naval staff had spotted an opportunity, a flaw in the Versailles Treaty and the Washington Naval Treaty of 1922. This flaw allowed them to build the so-called 'pocket battleships'. The first, the *Deutschland*, was launched in 1929. These pocket battleships were specifically designed as commerce raiders. They had two turrets of three 11-inch guns, carried fore and aft, and could sail at a top speed of 28 knots, and could carry fuel for a maximum range of over 21,000 miles. But although they were capable of such speed and range, and had such hitting power, they were only 600 feet in length and displaced only between 10,000 and 12,000 tons. They were formidable.

The problems of the navy were eased after Hitler came to power, since it received the funds which allowed it to carry out its construction plans, and after the Anglo-German Naval Treaty of June 1935, Germany could build up to 30 per cent of British naval tonnage in surface vessels and up to 45 per cent of British submarine tonnage, or the total equivalent tonnage of both these categories in submarines alone. Rear Admiral Karl Doenitz recommended that they should concentrate on submarines.

With hindsight, one can say that this suggestion was a simple stroke of genius, and if it had been accepted by Hitler it might have won him the war. Germany was not dependent on sea-borne commerce, having lost all its colonies. But Britain was so dependent. As it was, the U-boat activity in the Atlantic nearly brought Britain to its knees. If there had been more of these weapons, Britain might well have been starved out.

However, Doenitz's plan was not accepted. Raeder pushed ahead with his concept of a balanced fleet. When the war began, the Germans had two battleships, three pocket battle-ships and nine cruisers. An aircraft carrier, the *Graf Zeppelin*, was begun but never completed. Other ships were under construction, but in fact only two battleships, the *Bismarck* and the *Tirpitz*, and a cruiser, the *Prinz Eugen*, were completed. This was partly because the German navy had been told not to expect a war until 1944. As a result, when the war began, the German navy could not take on the Royal Navy, nor could it conduct a truly effective submarine campaign.

As a result, although the U-boats had some successes at the beginning of the war (they sank the aircraft carrier HMS *Courageous* in September 1939 and the battleship *Royal Oak* in Scapa Flow on 14 October) there was a problem. They could, at that time, hardly travel the long distance to the open Atlantic or remain there for very long. For this reason, the German surface vessels were more effective in raiding British shipping.

The Second World War is a wide area of study, but owing to the intense interest of academics and the public alike, most aspects of the conflict have been thoroughly documented. However, there are still aspects of the period which have received little or no attention. This is certainly true of the 'Hilfskreuzers' (auxiliary cruisers) of the German navy, which operated with devastating effect in the early part of the war. They wreaked havoc on British shipping, yet there is little appreciation of the danger they presented. The limelight has always been occupied by the submarine packs and their war in the North Atlantic. What were these 'Hilfskreuzers', or 'raiders', as we would call them?

There were less than a dozen in number – ordinary merchant ships converted into lethal mini-warships. They operated widely, one appearing in the North Atlantic, another in the South Atlantic – yet another would appear in the Indian Ocean to cause damage and fear thousands of miles away. They were limited in number, but sank almost a million tons of Allied shipping, mainly in the early war years. The trouble they caused was out of all proportion to their numbers. While it is true that they could not menace ships that were sailing in convoy, the convoy system was only of limited effectiveness. The Royal Navy did not have enough ships to protect each and every ship when they left their home port on the way to meet the convoy they were assigned to join. On that first leg of the journey they were vulnerable. The same applied to ships returning to the UK as they made their passage back to a convoy rendezvous point in West Africa, Newfoundland, or Halifax (Canada), for example, as well as after they left their convoy after reaching home waters.

Since the Germans (obviously) did not publicize these attacks, these disappearances must have, at first, been complete mysteries. However, the British naval command soon realized what was going on, and tried to send naval craft to the areas under threat. The problem was that they had limited resources, and every vessel detached to hunt down the raiders meant fewer effective escorts for the convoys. The Germans had a simpler job to do. Their merchant force was confined to harbour owing to British (and later Allied) naval strength. The Germans were obtaining their food supplies from the nations they had conquered. As a result German naval effort could go into attacking and harassing their enemy without worrying about protecting their own ships.

Another factor which kept information about the raiders to a minimum was that, in the main, the raiders had little opportunity to boast of their exploits, even if German Intelligence had allowed them to do so. They rarely came back to base, though after the fall of France an occasional raider might manage to slip back into some French port, now much more convenient than the German havens. Some of the raiders managed to dock in a friendly harbour (or at least a neutral one), in Spain, Italy or Japan, where their crew might journey back for a home leave. Also the Allies did not want to emphasize the problem, for two simple reasons. Firstly, they did not want to damage the morale of the merchant navy. Secondly, they did not want to alert the Germans to the fact that they were aware of what was going on.

As a result, ordinary merchant seamen heard very little about this danger. The author of *The Raider and the Tramp*, Alfred Lund, says:

> I am only able to take into consideration my own impressions of these raiders and have to admit that I knew or heard very little other than vague references to such vessels despite the fact that a ship I was serving in at that time (May to October 1940), which went to and fro on her voyage to Uruguay and Argentina without coming, apparently, near the *Widder* (one of the raiders) which was operating in the mid and North Atlantic section at that time. There was a reference made by one crew-member but no one connected it with a raider. We knew that the *Graf Spee* was lying scuttled in Montevideo Roads and surmised U-boats did not operate as far south at that time so we were at a loss to understand his unease.

In fact, one of the raiders, the *Thor*, was also operating in the mid- and South Atlantic, and had sunk six ships in that area in July 1940. Lund admits that it was just as well for his peace of mind that he did not know these unhappy facts.

The ordinary merchant captain and his crew were worried about battleships (pocket or otherwise), submarines, air attacks, and, to a lesser extent, mines – they did not know of the existence of the raiders for the most part.

What were these raiders, what were the problems they faced and how were they equipped? It was a task well outside the general thrust of ship construction in the German navy, whose main concern was the construction of U-boats and pocket battleships. When it came to the armed freighters that were to constitute the new raiding force, they presented the Germans with many difficulties during their fitting-out phase.

The armed merchant cruisers (AMCs) were the direct descendants of the privateers freely used by all nations in war in the late Middle Ages and later, right up to the 19th century.

They were also a feature of the First World War. In July 1914 various British shipping companies were told that some ships might be required to fulfil the role of AMCs should war be declared, and in the event famous liners like the *Aquitania*, the *Lusitania* and *Mauretania* were strengthened and armed ready for the role of operating in this capacity. They were not the only ones. Many other smaller vessels entered the war. One, the *Carmania*, became involved in an engagement with a German AMC and only just managed to scrape into Gibraltar for repairs.

Anybody interested in the naval history of the Second World War should consult K. Poolman's *Armed Merchant Cruisers*, an excellent and very full account of this aspect of the fighting.

In August 1939, just before the outbreak of the Second World War, a brief notice, similar to the one used in 1914, was served on various ship owners. Shaw Savill's *Jervis Bay*, P & O's *Rawalpindi*, the Royal Mail's liner *Asturias* and others were detailed to be transformed quickly into AMCs. One passenger ship, the *Dunvegan Castle*, was on the point of sailing from East London in South Africa when she was ordered into the war. All the passengers and baggage were promptly disembarked and she then sailed back to the UK for conversion. Sometimes these conversions were done too quickly, with dire results.

Probably the most important activity of these ships was their role as escorts to the numerous convoys both leaving and entering the war zones. As I have mentioned, however, their German opposite numbers had no merchant marine to protect. There were only a few of them, and they operated singly, endeavouring at all times to avoid combat with enemy armed vessels.

The conversion of merchant vessels to armed raiders is far from easy, and a number of authorities, including Poolman, Muggenthaler and Schmalenbach, have outlined the problems that confronted the shipyards. The main difficulty was that merchant ships are constructed for a different purpose and on a different plan to warships. Poolman's account is probably the most meticulous and explicit, and he draws on many reference sources. He points out that the Admiralty had shown great forethought by endeavouring to ensure that certain selected merchant ships should be constructed in ways which would enable them to be more easily converted to naval use in any future war.

The Germans started with a certain experience of the armed raider which dated back to the First World War. In that conflict, they used six light cruisers which succeeded in sinking about fifty merchant ships before being put out of action. They also equipped some fast liners with light armament, but these had drawbacks, principally their very high coal consumption, which raised refuelling problems, and they were easily recognizable as small passenger vessels.

During the Second World War, 12 raiders were ordered to be constructed on the orders of Admiral Raeder, the head of the German navy. This was to be done by converting cargo ships to this use. This order was put out very early in the war – November 1939 to be precise. He also ordered that a second group of raiders were to be made ready within the following six months. The ships chosen were cargo-type, oil-driven. This first wave of ships was not easy to convert. They were not new vessels, and were oil-fired, which limited them, since they were dependent on either obtaining fuel from supply ships or seizing oil from their victims, if possible.

The next difficulty was one of personnel. The typical European or American merchant vessel of the period was of between 3,000 and 8,000 tons, and had a crew of between 30 and 40, who lived in the forecastles and aftercastles while the deck and engineer officers and the catering staff lived amidships. However, the raiders needed to carry a much larger crew. They required approximately 400 crewmen. They needed not only the seamen who were required to navigate the vessel, but also repair and maintenance engineers, gun crew, medical personnel, and many other trained men, such as radio operators, machinists, range-finder personnel, and pilots for the planes which were carried.

To accommodate all these men was very difficult. In addition, the ship had to carry extensive armament to fulfil its function of commerce raiding, and the armament had to be concealed yet capable of being brought into action very rapidly. This problem was overcome in various ways. The guns were concealed behind sliding shutters or under such disguises as mock-ups of cable drums, or locomotive fire-boxes. Aboard one of the raiders, the *Wolf*, the torpedoes were fired from tubes on deck, part of the bulwark being hinged to swing downwards when launching the weapon. The torpedo was aimed by an improvised gun-sight mechanism, which was aimed at the target after its speed was taken into account.

In addition, each ship had to carry a crew of specialists who were employed to change the appearance of the vessel when circumstances dictated a new identity. These changes were extensive – they had to be. For example, a vessel might be seen by an Allied plane or ship with sansom-posts, the colours of a real shipping line, and a certain profile of deck-houses, and proceeding due north at a usual speed, perhaps eight to ten knots. A few days later, the same plane, or the same ship, might be checking a nearby stretch of sea and spot another freighter, now heading west, but bearing no similarities to the ship seen earlier. In order to carry out these changes effectively, the raiders had to have a detailed knowledge of the customs and usages of the numerous shipping lines of the world. One line might be distinguished for the sloppy appearance of its vessels. Another line might have always favoured a particular shipbuilder, the characteristics of whose work could be easily noted. Also, the raider had to be careful not to appear too alert and seamanlike. Merchant ships were expected to be slow to answer signals, and to make mistakes.

The 'cosmetic surgeons' who altered the ships' appearance had to be ready to alter the position of masts, derrick posts and lifeboats. The bulwarks might have to be raised, using metal sheeting. Funnel markings would have to be changed, and the whole ship repainted. Naval ships expected neutrals to have their names, port of registry and national flags painted on their sides. All this raised tremendous difficulties, and the deception had to be exact. The slightest error in detail could give a ship away. The German raider *Pinguin* was caught because a British spotter plane noticed that she had no black men among the crew visible on her decks. A British ship of the time would inevitably feature a crew of mixed racial origins.

However, the careful work of the camouflage and deception parties generally worked. If the suspect vessel was inspected by a plane, the pilot was often not sufficiently suspicious to make more than a cursory inspection, or if a warship was involved, it would only seldom bother to come alongside for closer scrutiny. Even then, it was difficult to be sure, and the vessel concerned was often in a hurry. Let us look at an example mentioned by Muggenthaler.

On this occasion, the *City of Exeter* after such a sighting reported back to Naval Command that they considered the *Kasii Maru* (apparently a Japanese freighter sailing prior to Japan's entry into the war) 'looked suspicious' but as the *City of Exeter* was on a demanding homeward bound trip she did not stop. The disguised freighter was in fact, the raider *Atlantis*, the most successful raider in terms of gross tonnage sunk or captured. To add to the deception, the captain (Rogge) instructed his officer on watch at the time to don a kimono as he paraded the bridge. To give added effect the 'wife' (a small dark-haired lad), suitably clad, could be seen pushing a baby carriage down on the weather deck.

Muggenthaler's report suggested that the *City of Exeter* was an armed surveillance vessel was confusing and thus could have been attacked by Captain Rogge. D. Davidson, mentioned in Lund's book, asserted that the ship was never anything other than a passenger liner and furthermore was never classified as an AMC although the encounter with the *Atlantis* was as reported.

Muggenthaler (who had German affiliations) uses the facts to demonstrate the efficiency of the German disguise technique. But it was reported by K. Poolman that Rogge had his own reasons for avoiding action at the time.

Poolman states in his book *Armed Merchant Cruisers* that Rogge knew that the *City of Exeter*, returning to the UK, had a full cargo of passengers. As he was heading for his operational zone in the Indian Ocean, to sink her would have actually hampered the *Atlantis* in carrying out her orders. Rogge was not a sadistic or cruel man, unlike some raider captains, and if he had sunk her he would have been more inclined to have taken them (at least in the case of the passengers) aboard his ship, rather than leave them stranded in mid-Atlantic – so he probably just decided to continue as a Japanese neutral.

I now return to the matter of the physical preparation of the ships. Armament was naturally a very high priority. It has already been mentioned that this had to be concealed – but it also had to be adequate in terms of firepower. The raiders depended on strength to ensure that the merchant ships could be overwhelmed and prevented, not only from resisting, but also from sending out signals for help, and this had to be done within a few seconds. Even though the merchantmen were threatened with instant destruction if anyone used their radios, as the war went on, more and more vessels, when waylaid, made signals in spite of the risk (and an almost certain risk at that) of instant death.

Just how formidable the raiders were is shown by the exploit of the *Kormoran*. This raider fought a ship-to-ship duel with HMAS *Sydney*, a light cruiser, off West Australia on 19 November 1941. The *Kormoran* was destroyed, and her lifeboats were launched and eventually most of the crew were rescued and survived. But the *Sydney* disappeared. She and her crew of 645 were never seen again. Details of this fight are given in a subsequent chapter [p. 60].

Other lighter weapons included a 21-inch torpedo tube and machine guns, with searchlights, and range finders, all of which had to be camouflaged. All guns had to be very carefully placed so as to give them a maximum range of fire. The decks had to be strengthened to support the weight of the guns, and to stand up to the shock of their recoil. The guns had to be serviced with ammunition hoists and storage rooms, which had to be as close as possible to the gun-sites. This was vital because for the ships to operate efficiently all their fire-power had to be available quickly. In addition, two of the raiders also carried mine-laying motor-boats and the *Michel* also had a motor torpedo boat on board.

The folding deckhouses and false bulwarks had to be made so as to give maximum efficiency when any action commenced. The gun ports were covered with slatted, hinged flaps from which the raider could open fire very quickly whether by day or night or whatever the weather. As a necessary adjunct to the arrangements made to change the appearance of the ship frequently and efficiently, such things as collapsible ventilators, removable king posts, and funnels and masts that could reduce telescopically in a few minutes, had to be provided and fitted, and the crew had to be sure that they would work perfectly. All this structural equipment took up a lot of space. Again in the name of disguise, tons of paint had to be carried and a large number of rubber boats stowed so as to be immediately accessible in an emergency. These had to be concealed because the 'official' lifeboats which each ship carried had to be very limited in number – completely insufficient to accommodate the hundreds of men on board.

To preserve the appearance of normality under scrutiny, attention to detail was all-important. The crew was forbidden to stroll freely on deck – again, to guard against arousing suspicion if a ship or plane inspected the raider. This was, in fact, all-important, since an inspection of an average merchant vessel of the type which the raiders were imitating would normally see nobody on deck apart from the officer of the watch and three or four workers doing such jobs as hosing down, chipping rust, or painting. In fact, they always had to be on the watch for danger. At any time a submarine could surface nearby, or a scouting plane from a ship over the horizon would suddenly appear. Of course, the same applied to the hundreds of unarmed cargo ships which were sailing on what up to then had been peaceful seas.

The raider ships carried one or two planes (which were Heinkel 114B seaplanes). The pilots did not find these totally satisfactory for landings and take-offs while at sea, and the flying officers of one of the raiders, the *Atlantis*, asked for improvements, but were told that the particular plane they asked for, the Arado 196, was needed for the *Graf Spee*. Of course, they knew that this was an excuse – the *Graf Spee* had either been sunk by the British or scuttled, but this was never admittedly publicly because it was too big a blow to German morale.

These planes had to be accommodated somewhere, along with all the other equipment and personnel which every raider had to carry. One would think that a freighter would have plenty of space going begging, but this was not the case. The only truly spare space was in the holds – of which there were at least five. The planes had to be stowed there, but difficulties still remained. The planes had to be well out of sight, but it was also essential that they could be brought rapidly up to deck level when needed, and could be stowed away just as quickly. They took up a great deal of room, and since the space above them had to be kept clear, the only other use the lower part of holds they occupied could be put to was the stowage of the many spare parts the ship needed, such as machine spares, gun replacements and thousands of duplicate accessories of some kind. Another use for the lower part of the holds was the storage of fresh water supplies and extra oil-storage tanks. (Oil posed unique problems generally).

The main use of the planes was for reconnaissance. The raider's main concern was to avoid detection, and a plane could help enormously in this respect, but another use was to detect possible targets. When a suitable ship was spotted, the plane could either shadow it until the mother-ship caught up, or return with a report. The pressure of war gave rise to continual improvement in techniques. Sometimes the aircraft would drop a bag on the target with instructions to make its way towards its new master, and reinforce these orders with a bomb or a burst of machine gun fire. Some pilots actually used a trailing, weighted length of wire to rip away the radio aerial of the target vessel, to prevent appeals for rescue.

Sometimes these reconnaissance flights experienced difficulty, owing to the planes experiencing navigational problems and being unable to find their way back. The pilots had to plot their positions relative to the mother-ship using dead reckoning, but this sometimes broke down. However, in an emergency the mother-ship could always put out a radio signal which the pilot could use as a homing device.

This brings up the question of supply, which was vital for a raider far from home. There was a well-organized fleet of supply ships, which had to seek out their target in remote parts of the globe and hand over their cargo. This worked well, for the most part, but if more supplies were expended than expected, problems could arise. Oil was one of the most difficult problems. Water could be obtained from remote islands, but oil was a constant problem. (Of course, the raiders could have called at neutral ports, relying on their disguise, and purchased oil and taken on fresh water there. But the worry always was that such visits might have provided invaluable opportunities to Allied Intelligence, and so this course was never adopted.)

One solution was to take fuel from captured ships, and this was done whenever possible. But modern engines are sensitive to the chemical composition of the oil used. With this in mind, a sample of the oil captured, whether from a tanker or from a captured vessel, had to be analysed to see if it was suitable for use. If it was, then the oil had to be transferred, which was a major problem in itself. If the oil was just for lubrication purposes, there was less difficulty. Lubricating oil was generally kept in drums, but boiler or diesel oil would have to be pumped aboard using a pipeline.

This in turn would mean that the raider would have to moor alongside the captured vessel. A 'messenger' line would be fired across by rocket, and then used to pull over a thick towline. An alternative was for the crew to haul aboard a line which would be used to pull over an oil pipeline attached to a floating line, which would keep the pipeline above water. The closed end of this pipeline would be taken on board the captured vessel and connected to a valve leading to the oil storage system. The oil could then be pumped across. When that had been finished, the oil pipe would be hauled back aboard the raider. It would then be 'run in'. That is, the men handling it would haul the pipe back over the bow, and run aft with it to uncouple it from the stand-pipe which led the oil down into the storage tanks. If the transfer was being made from a German navy supply ship, the oil would come over the stern of the raider, because the navy tanker would have more room to lay out the piping.

This was an extremely ticklish and difficult business. Both ships had to keep together, and adjustment had to be made for different rates of drift. Otherwise, the connecting lines and the oil pipe would sever, pulled apart by the weight of the ships. Not only that, but it had to be done quickly. These difficulties were compounded if the weather was really bad. In these cases both ships would have to steam into the prevailing seas, just maintaining steerage way, while the transfer was being carried out. But it could be done. In September 1939 the naval oil transport *Nordmark* refuelled the pocket battleship *Deutschland* in a storm with Force 12 wind and Force 9 sea.

Supplies other than oil, such as food and ammunition, presented fewer problems, and sometimes the supply ship and the cruiser could lie side by side (weather conditions permitting), which eased the whole difficulty considerably. Vigilance had to be constantly exercised. A leak in an oil pipeline could give rise to a tell-tale patch of oil, and supplies dropped overboard could also give clues to a searching naval ship.

There was at least one occasion when a raider was surprised when refuelling, which is examined in detail in the account of Captain Bernhard Rogge's exploits. Captain Rogge lost his ship as a result. Sometimes rendezvous had to be made in a port, when bulky supplies such as heavy machine parts or aircraft had to be handed over, loads which would be difficult or impossible to transfer at sea.

One of the greatest problems the crew suffered was simply that of overcrowding. As I have mentioned, the hulls of the raider ships were crammed with supplies and with additional crew members. As a result of this overcrowding, crew quarters were dire – cramped, stuffy and often damp. Food was very monotonous, and the supply ships often omitted to bring fresh vegetables, fruit or bottled beer. The result was a great deal of grumbling among the crews.

The overcrowding was exacerbated when prisoners were taken. The strangers had to be guarded, fed, and tended. It must have been tempting, sometimes, to think of just releasing them. But apart from the fact that trained seamen (who formed the bulk of such prisoners) were a great asset to the Allies, there was always the fear that released prisoners might have gained useful information during their time on the raider ships. This was especially dangerous in the case of merchant navy officers, who could use their experience to put together a good deal of vital information. Captain Bernhard Rogge, described in detail later, was especially wily in overcoming this tendency. He would actually provide a false picture of events for his prisoners to store away. At one point, for example, when his ship was actually concerned with mine-laying off the coast of South America, he provided audio camouflage to suggest that he was tied up alongside a U-boat.

In spite of all these problems, Muggenthaler's report states that courage, endurance and morale among the crews was high. That seems remarkable, since every day could be the day when they would see an end to their raiding – and to their lives. Many of the voyages combined the worst of both worlds. Discomfort and boredom accompanied by constant fear.

Even so, one raider crew managed to survive 622 days of action at sea – pouncing on lone victims like 'a fox on geese' as Reserve Lieutenant Commander Helmuth von Ruckteschell remarked.

They never knew where their enemy was – radio signal might come from just over the horizon or hundreds of miles away. To add to the uncertainty, they could not decode such signals – at least, not fully. This did change after the attack on the *Automedon* in early November 1940. The new code was found on board her and used until changes were made, as Muggenthaler makes clear. However, there were variations among the crew, and it seemed that the large portion of the crew who were on the young side and without family responsibilities endured the voyages better than the older men, who often showed the traumatic effects of the stressful situation they were in.

This is a good place to say something about the crews. They were a mixture of German naval personnel as well as merchant seamen. This mixture gave rise to problems, probably because of the looser discipline to which the merchant seamen were accustomed. Rogge, one of the raider commanders, quickly formed the opinion that a large number of his allotted hands were not what he desired, and got rid of them before sailing.

Muggenthaler questioned Captain J. Armstrong White, OBE. Captain White's ship, the *City of Baghdad*, was sunk by the raider *Atlantis*. White said of himself that he 'was very British and not pro-German' but said that it was 'only fair to describe Rogge (who commanded the *Atlantis*) as a nice fellow with good human qualities of decency and honour'.

The raider captains were, indeed, often extremely ruthless. The ethics of warfare form a complicated and emotional source of endless argument, and it is futile to explore such a matter in detail here. However, in fairness it should be remembered that war, by whoever it happens to be waged, is a ruthless business. In the case of the raiders, sheer self-preservation dictated that their first motto had to be 'Kill or be killed'. If they were to achieve the aims laid down for them by the High Command, that was how it would have to be. Nonetheless, there were variations in basic ethical attitudes among the captains, as will be shown later.

Admiral Raeder, the naval commander in chief, knew very well that the trade by sea was potentially Britain's most vulnerable spot. Sixty-eight million tons of freight reached her every year in a merchant navy which possessed 21 million tons of cargo capacity. If that could be destroyed, the war could well be won by virtue of that fact alone. The raider captains were told to destroy British merchant ships wherever they could be found. It was thought that a side effect of this would be to force the dispersal of the Royal Navy's craft very widely (presumably thus preventing their concentration against Germany for any reason) and disrupt shipping movements generally. Another effect of this, they hoped, would be that their own battleships would find it easier to operate.

To do all this, the raiders had first to attain access to the North Atlantic, where the heaviest streams of British shipping were to be found, carrying war munitions and essential supplies of all kinds between America and their homeland. In the early part of the war, the raiders found it fairly easy to get into the North Atlantic area. Once inside, they had varying success in carrying out their missions.

We now have to consider the geography as it affected the situation. The British Isles form a long barrier across the North Sea, and this barrier allowed naval forces using British ports to command all the German sea-routes into the major oceans. The sea passage between the north of Britain and Greenland is split by the Faroes and Iceland, which helped the British by providing choke points which the raiders and the German battleships had to use. Very often they chose the more remote route, which offered less danger, as the fog, snow and other bad weather conditions enabled them to proceed unnoticed into the Atlantic north-western approaches without detection.

When France capitulated, the prospects for the German sea-war received an enormous boost. The Germans now controlled the northern and western coasts of France, and thus were able to establish bases for U-boats, battleships and their raiders. Not all of the latter, however, chose to take this route. Quite a few of them left Kiel and sailed along the Norwegian coast, which provided some shelter because of the numerous islands, fjords and sea channels which provided a fairly safe route to the North Atlantic. Sometimes the raiders made their way out south of Iceland, and went either north or west of the Faroes and Shetland Islands. Nevertheless, the capture of France was very important, and the raiders *Michel, Thor, Komet,* and *Stier* were able to sneak down past the Dutch and French coasts and down to northern Spain before they launched out on their missions against the British shipping.

The Germans constructed pens for their U-boats at St Nazaire, a very successful move, whose success endured until the Allies' bombing capacity increased later in the war, and this port was also used by the raiders. Brest, Lorient and La Rochelle provided safe havens for the raiders when they returned from the Atlantic, unless they preferred, as some captains did, to come back by the northern route described above, which was somewhat safer.

The essence of the matter was that it allowed the raiders a larger sphere of operations, which was key to their success. It is often not appreciated how vast the oceans are, and how difficult it is to find a ship lost in them. How much more difficult, then, when the ship you are looking for constantly changes its appearance and course. In fact, this problem affected the raiders themselves. Very often they wandered for long periods through an empty waste of waters. All this time they were consuming food and fuel, and thus supply was one of their central problems. Of course, if the raider went into action, it would expend ammunition, and this had to be replaced as well. This meant that the raiders had to be backed up with a flotilla of supply ships and since the Allies would regard such supply ships as combatants, the supply ships had to use the same disguises and subterfuges as the raiders themselves. A number of suitable merchant ships of varying sizes were pressed into service for this purpose.

Another task which the supply ships carried out was to carry away any prisoners the raiders took. Such prisoners were a nuisance, since they had to be guarded and fed aboard a ship where there was very little space to spare.

Prisoners and their capture represented a constant problem, and sometimes the raiders actually captured one of their prey instead of sinking it, and turned it into a prison ship. Rogge himself captured a Yugoslavian ship called the *Durmitor* at one point. She was a really filthy old ship, filled with rats and cockroaches, and truly deserved the name of 'tramp' steamer. Rogge apologized to the prisoners for putting them on board her. He could only spare limited provisions and the prisoners had to sleep on top of the cargo she was carrying. It was salt, and made a cold and clammy bed.

Two hundred and ninety-nine prisoners were put on board, and were soon filled with hate for their captors, so miserable were their conditions. There was a German prize crew aboard, a mere two officers and twelve men. Water rationing was put in force and then they also found that the coal aboard was insufficient for them to maintain a good speed. If they wanted to make port they had to steam slowly, which drew out the discomfort. Food had to be rationed too, and there was very nearly a mutiny. These appalling conditions were inflicted by one of the best raider captains, though in his defence one must admit that it was a practical necessity.

It is worth noting another little-known incident in regard to a better known raider, the *Graf Spee*. Her supply ship was called the *Altmark*, which was spotted proceeding southwards through the territorial waters of Norway, bound for Germany. She was known to have three hundred British prisoners on board, having evaded the British naval blockade on the way back from the Atlantic. Norwegian naval officers inspected her, but found no sign of prisoners and noted that the ship was not armed. Under international law, she had to be allowed to proceed on her way. However, Churchill was confident that the prisoners were on board, and ordered HMS *Cossack*, a destroyer, to go into Norwegian naval waters, board the *Altmark* and release the prisoners. (It is said that this was brought about by a covert Morse torchlight signal by one of the prisoners through a porthole on the *Altmark*, but the truth of the matter is uncertain.) In any event, Captain Philip Vian of the *Cossack* had no great difficulty in stopping the *Altmark* and found the prisoners locked up in storerooms and an empty oil tank.

It may be that this rescue influenced Hitler's decision to attack Denmark and Norway in April 1940.

The supply ships were dealt with ruthlessly by the Royal Navy, which insisted on searching any ship which appeared suspicious, whatever its apparent nationality. Many others were sunk by naval craft or by bombing. Still others scuttled themselves when the navy appeared and wished to search them.

In the course of this vigilance, other opportunities presented themselves. In one case, a French naval sloop obedient to the Vichy government was escorting six Vichy merchant vessels from Indo-China. They were carrying valuable cargoes which were destined for use by the German Reich.

HMS *Devonshire* and three other ships intercepted them in the Indian Ocean. Boarding parties were placed aboard all the ships very rapidly, and prevented the pro-Nazi crews from scuttling the ships, though one managed to damage her engines and another destroyed her steering gear. However, in spite of these efforts, they were taken over by the boarding parties and sailed to Durban. After the initial trouble, the crews offered very little resistance.

It must be admitted that they helped considerably to upset normal shipping arrangements. Partly because of them, all British ships had to move in convoys, escorted by naval vessels. To do this effectively, the British had to set up convoy collection points. At any one time, numbers of ships would be anchored waiting for their convoy, perhaps with cargo already aboard, in places such as the Forth, the Clyde, Loch Ewe and Loch Long in Scotland, Milford Haven in Wales, and also in various other estuaries and lochs around British shores.

Not only this, they had to wait for convoys to take them back, in such places as Freetown, West Africa, in Nova Scotia, Gibraltar, Newfoundland and many other safe areas which formed gathering points. This caused many delays. Ships could wait weeks for appropriate escort arrangements in a convoy where their speed fitted in with the rest of the 'customers'. There were eight-, nine- and ten-knot convoys, and if a ship could not keep up with the rest, she could not join.

The German strategy also succeeded in dispersing Royal Navy craft as soon as the British became aware of raider activity. Sending ships to an area where the raiders were known to be prowling was the only way to contain and minimize shipping losses. To attain these objectives, the general tactics of the raiders were a foregone conclusion, dictated by the situation they had to confront. The Hilfskreuzers' directives were quite exact and the commanders of the vessels used whatever methods were needed to carry them out, whether fair or foul.

The raiders operated by approaching the merchant ship they had targeted, still disguised. They then abandoned the disguise at the latest possible moment, and radioed or signalled the hapless vessel to heave-to. If the ship in question tried to send out a radio signal, the raider would immediately shell the bridge area, since that was where the radio cabin was located. Sometimes these cabins were protected by sandbags or by an extra skin of concrete blocks buckled around them. However, these precautions were usually useless, and the radio operators were generally killed, with anyone else in the bridge area sharing their fate.

British Naval Control had set up a series of signals which the ships could send if the operator dared. 'QQQQ' meant that the ship was being attacked by an armed merchant raider. 'RRRR' meant they were being attacked by a battleship, while 'SSSS' indicated a submarine was involved. It was obviously desirable that they give their position, but if they could not, it was possible that Naval Control had a general idea of their whereabouts through their knowledge of shipping movements, for all voyages were notified to them. However, an exact position had many advantages – it enabled a more effective pursuit of the raider, and it afforded the crew a better chance of being picked up with a rescue craft. As I have mentioned, many ships did send such messages when under attack – a very brave act when you remember that sending such a message invited immediate death for the sender.

From the German point of view, it was essential that their whereabouts remained secret. If a message got through, not only would an avenger be on their tail, but the pursuer would know what to look for, and naturally the warning would go out to all other merchant ships. The Germans knew, too, that they were regarded in a different light to the regular navy. They would be unlikely to receive much consideration or mercy so to be ruthless was merely to protect themselves. Nevertheless, many people regarded such a one-sided conflict as straightforward murder, and it is true that some raider captains were guilty of very brutal actions.

This is a good place to refer to the sinking of the British passenger liner *Britannia* by the German raider *Thor*, which was commanded by Captain Kahler. The facts recorded here come from Muggenthaler's *German Raiders of World War II*, a very detailed, well-researched account of the raiders and their war.

There were over 500 passengers and crew on the *Britannia*, including at least 12 women (see Lund's *The Raider and the Tramp*). After the sinking, the lucky ones were left adrift in one of the nine lifeboats. One of these had 82 men in it. The unlucky ones were on rafts or bits of debris or even floating in their life-belts. The only thing that can be said in favour of the *Thor* is that the crew did wait until the passengers were all off before sinking the *Britannia*, but they left them in terrible conditions.

Muggenthaler's account is mainly excellent, but there is one point about which there seems to be doubt. When he looked into the German point of view on the subject, he found some pleas in mitigation of what was done. One of the excuses was a supposed radio signal from an unnamed British naval ship 112 miles away. This was (again, supposedly) decoded by the German radio officer, and the German view was that this decided them to leave without giving further aid, assuming that the British ship would look after her own 'within an hour'. Mr Lund, who investigated the matter, could not substantiate this signal, and pointed out that no ship could cover that distance in only one hour. It may be that Muggenthaler's German sympathies influenced his account.

Muggenthaler does report that the crew of the German ship saw the sea covered in burning oil, and sharks cruising around the survivors before they left, and that they were rather quiet as they ate their meal afterwards. The details of the plight of the survivors can be relied on, since they were supplied to Muggenthaler by William MacVicar, the third officer of the *Britannia*. In spite of the appalling conditions, 331 people did survive the disaster, which is remarkable when one considers that they were almost on the equator, and suffered from dehydration and extreme heat as well as hunger and thirst.

Perhaps the only comment to be made on the matter is that the incident was an example of the appalling things that happen once war is a fact, and, as the Romans said, 'The laws sleep among the weapons'. Although this happened under a Nazi government, atrocities just as bad happened in the First World War, before Nazism existed.

Rucktheschell, on the *Michel*, avoided the problems posed by prisoners by the simple expedient of not taking any. The *Anglo Saxon*, whose destruction is described in detail later, was far from being the only massacre he carried out. The *Lylepark* (Denholme's Line) was blown into smithereens at close quarters on 11 June 1942. On 15 July, a few days later, he attacked and sank the *Gloucester Castle* (Union Castle Line). She was built in 1911, and was the smallest and oldest ship owned by Union Castle. There were 154 people on board, bound for South Africa. She sank quickly, in only four minutes, and there was no time to get into the lifeboats. Eighty-two, including six women and two children, were drowned or died in the heavy shelling which tore apart the superstructure.

3   The sinking of the Athenia

At around 7.30 p.m. on 3 September 1939, Kapitänleutnant Fritz-Julius Lemp, commanding *U-30*, sighted what he identified as a British merchantman south of Rockall. Lemp fired two torpedoes, hitting the target, which turned out to be the 13,500-ton Donaldson liner *Athenia*. Among the 122 passengers who perished were 28 Americans, which caused acute embarrassment to German U-boat Kapitän zur See Karl Doenitz. He had already deployed 80 per cent of his ocean-going submarines around Britain. As Lemp had kept radio silence, the German propaganda machine attempted to switch the blame, claiming *Athenia* had been sunk by the British.

Hitler's orders had specifically stated that submarine warfare was to be waged according to the terms of the Hague Convention Prize Regulations. Doenitz immediately organized an investigation into the incident. The day after the sinking, Doenitz signalled his crews that existing orders for mercantile warfare remained in force. This was reinforced several hours later by a further signal: 'By order of the Fuhrer passenger ships will not be attacked, even if in convoy, until further notice.'

The *Athenia* had left the Clyde the previous Friday packed with civilians of all nationalities fleeing the impending war. The vessel was bound for Montreal and Quebec, where she was due to arrive the following Sunday. The *U-30* was among a number of U-boats that had left their bases in Germany during the last week of August. Lemp, a 26-year-old professional officer, was patrolling slowly with his vessel, when a lookout in the conning-tower sighted a large merchant ship proceeding westward on a zig-zag course. Without wasting any time, *U-30* dived to take up an attacking position.

Of the two torpedoes fired at almost point-blank range by *U-30*, one found its target on *Athenia*'s port side, ripping the boiler room and engine-room apart. The stairs from the third-class and tourist dining saloons were also destroyed, making it impossible for passengers to escape. Launching the lifeboats on the starboard side proved difficult as the vessel quickly developed a list of thirty degrees to port, but miraculously the liner somehow settled in the water to remain afloat for several hours. This enabled all the lifeboats to be lowered.

Tom Ritchie, of Glasgow, who was a 19-year-old assistant steward at the time recalls:

> It was exactly 7.40 p.m. when the torpedo struck. It was light outside, but dark inside the ship because of the 'deadlights' over the portholes. We were serving the evening meal and

I was in the pantry when there was this enormous explosion followed by a sensation of great heat.

All the lights went out immediately and everything was in total darkness. It was all right for the crew for we knew our way about the ship blindfolded. But when I came out of the pantry into the dining room there was screaming and panic.

Some of the pipes on the deckheads burst and were spurting oil. Everyone knows the mess seabirds get into with oil spillages. Well, that's what we were like as we found our way across the dining room to a companionway. But the first staircase we came to had been blown off and we had to climb to the deck above by little ledges. It was our duty to get to the lifeboats as quick as we could in an emergency. Each man had a specific task so the boat could be made ready and lowered as safely as possible and with the right number of passengers.

I climbed into my boat and we were loading it with women and children but we were being hindered by groups of male passengers, all very excited and panicking. They were shoving the women and kids aside and trying to scramble on the boats.

Each lifeboat carries a couple of axes and I grabbed one. I'm only 5ft 3in but I must have looked a bit menacing for I shouted at the men 'The first one to come on this boat will get his leg chopped off.' They backed off and we got loaded up with women and children.

The complement of my boat was 80. We have over 100 on it, but it was all right and we made the water okay, which thankfully was calm and the weather was mild. But that didn't help the women, many of whom were in nightwear, having gone to bed early.

I didn't get any time to see my dad, who was a saloon steward with a different lifeboat station. Anyway I hoped he would be okay and not hurt in the initial explosion. When we got into the water we started rowing as hard as we could away from the ship, and when I looked back she appeared to be going down by the stern. We were unable to pick up any more survivors for if we had we would have sunk too. We rowed for hours before sighting a ship.

When we got nearer we could see a glow . . . it was the Norwegian flag painted on her sides and lit up. We could see her picking up survivors and we headed towards her. But after an hour and a half of hard rowing we were no nearer. The sea was running against us and it seemed we were taking two steps forward and three back.

We kept rowing right through the night. Lifeboats in those days used to take on lots of water and we were up to our knees in it, so much of the time was spent bailing out. The women got their shoes off and were bailing out with them. They were really wonderful. They calmed the kids who had been frightened . . . they calmed everyone and kept our spirits up.

It was about 4.30 in the morning and we were still rowing away when suddenly a searchlight was put on us from a ship nearby. We hadn't seen it until then and thought it was the U-boat that had sunk us. But it was a Swedish millionaire's yacht. He owned Electrolux and was on a cruise to Miami.

We were hauled on board and a big Swede helped me, put a woollen jumper over my shoulders, gave me a packet of Lucky Strike cigarettes and told me to go down to the lounge and get a cup of hot soup.

I could have passed out when I looked up at the man who was serving the soup . . . it was my dad. We grabbed each other and hugged, both of us overjoyed that the other had been saved.

The following morning two British destroyers came alongside and one of them had its decks covered with the bodies they had picked up from our ship. Each one was covered with a Union Jack. We were taken off the yacht and as we headed back to Scotland we came upon the *Athenia* . . . she was still afloat and listing that same way at the stern.

The destroyers stopped and were getting ready to set their guns in order to sink her when she seemed to tip right up into a perpendicular position and went straight down. It had been a peculiar sensation seeing her again and brought a big lump to my throat. She had been our home and our workplace and she was . . . going down.

We were landed at Greenock the next morning. From there we were taken to Glasgow for a slap-up meal at the old Beresford Hotel, now the Baird Hall in Sauchiehall Street. The crew were each given £5 from the shipping company . . . who later deducted it from our wages!

After the meal we met a young gentleman from London to see the American survivors. I'll always remember him . . . he was a lovely chap and seemed genuinely interested as he spoke to us about our ordeal. He was . . . John F. Kennedy. His father, Joe, was American Ambassador at the time and he had been over living with him in London.

Within a few days of the sinking, the Nazi-controlled press claimed that the British had torpedoed their own ship in order to provoke the United States into entering the war. On 16 September, at the instigation of Ribbentrop, Admiral Raeder invited the American naval attaché for talks in Berlin. Raeder stated that he had now received records from all of his U-boat commanders which indicated that the *Athenia* had not been sunk by a German U-boat. The attaché quickly informed Washington of Raeder's findings. However, the Grand Admiral's utterances were later found to be disingenuous. Not all the submarines which were at sea on 3 September had yet returned to port. Included among those was the *U-30*, commanded by Oberleutnant Lemp.

Later, at his trial in Nuremburg, Raeder outlined in detail his meeting with Lemp as *U-30* returned to Wilhelmshaven harbour on 27 September. After asking to meet him privately, said Raeder, Lemp had admitted to him that he had been responsible for sinking the *Athenia*. He had mistaken the liner for an armed merchant cruiser on patrol. It later became known that Raeder himself had ordered that the *Athenia* affair be kept secret. He insisted that any mention of the sinking was to be deleted from *U-30*'s log. He also swore the vessel's crew to absolute secrecy. The High Commander of the German navy decreed that a court-martial was not necessary, as they were satisfied that Lemp had acted in good faith. Lemp was later transferred to *U-110* and went down with her on 9 May 1941, following an encounter with the destroyers HMS *Bulldog* and HMS *Broadway*.

4   Where is the *Ark Royal*?

On 26 September three British warships were steering westward across the North Sea, escorting a damaged submarine back to port. They were His Majesty's battleships *Nelson* and *Rodney* and the aircraft carrier *Ark Royal*, steaming in close order behind their destroyer escort. The *Ark Royal* was launched on Merseyside on 13 April 1937 at a cost of £2,335,000 making hers the most valuable contract the Admiralty had awarded since the end of the First World War.

She had nine decks and her iron flight deck was 800 feet in length, with a beam of 94 feet. The ship's armament consisted of 16 4.5 inch guns, four multiple pom-poms, and eight multiple machine guns. Her speed was 30.75 knots and her fuel endurance exceeded that of any other previous aircraft carrier. She carried 60 aircraft: five Fleet Air Arm squadrons composed of Blackburn Skuas and Fairey Swordfish. The Swordfish were two-seater dive-bombers with a speed of 200 mph. They were capable of carrying a 500 lb bomb-load.

Two of the *Ark Royal* reconnaissance aircraft were on patrol over the ships. It was a bright morning with excellent visibility. For a long time the Fleet Air Arm men saw nothing unusual, then at 10.45 a.m. one of them sighted, some ten miles away to the south-east, three Dornier Do 18 flying-boats shadowing the British fleet.

The *Ark Royal* received confirmation of the Luftwaffe's presence and the crew was ordered to 'Action Stations'. The aircraft carrier turned into wind and dispatched nine Blackburn Skuas, which, in fact, were slower than the Luftwaffe flying-boats they were to attack.

It was the moment the pilots had been waiting for for almost three weeks – the first Fleet Air Arm combat of the war. The first section formed up over the *Ark Royal*, to be followed at intervals by the second and third sections, and they then flew into the attack. The enemy flying-boats kept low over the sea, their dark-blue and green camouflage making it difficult for the Skuas to locate them. At last, each section found its target and attacked. Although the Dorniers were heavily armed, two of them retired damaged, their superior speed ensuring their escape. The third was shot down by Lieutenant B. S. McEwen and his air gunner, Acting Petty Officer Airman B. M. Seymour. The naval airmen claimed the first enemy aircraft to be destroyed by British forces during the war. HMS *Somali*, an escort destroyer, picked up the Dornier crew of four and sank the flying-boat. Meanwhile, the surviving Dorniers had already reported the position of the British naval force and had alerted a German attacking force from Westerland, on the Frisian island of Sylt.

Within an hour after the last Skua had landed back on the *Ark Royal*, a Ju 88 approached the carrier under cloud cover at a height of 6,000 feet. Diving steeply from stern to bow, it released a 2,000 lb bomb before roaring away in a climbing turn. The officers on the bridge of the *Ark Royal* watched the bomb come spiralling down towards the ship. One of them thought it looked like an Austin Seven car. Another reported that it looked more like a London bus! The captain gave an order to alter course and as the ship turned away to starboard, the bomb exploded. It landed in the sea some 30 yards off the bow causing a cascade of water to shower the flight deck. The carrier reared her bow and plunged down again. The only damage to the ship was some broken crockery in the galley. The bomber swooped back over the flight deck spraying it with machine gun fire, before making its escape.

The German pilot, Leutnant Karl Francke, reported that he had dive-bombed the *Ark Royal* but did not, in fact, claim to have sunk her. However, Josef Goebbels, at the Ministry of Propaganda, made the claim for him. The next morning the newspapers throughout Nazi Germany proclaimed the loss of the *Ark Royal*. Field Marshal Goering sent Francke a telegram of congratulations, decorated him with the Iron Cross and promoted him to the rank of Oberleutnant.

It soon became apparent, however, that the German High Command's claims did not deceive Francke's fellow officers. They knew he was unworthy of the decoration and the fame he had received, and he soon became the laughing stock of the Luftwaffe. Francke was so tormented by the ridicule that he decided the only way to protect the honour of his family was to commit suicide. An American journalist, William Bayles, suggested that he denounce the Ministry of Propaganda and forget suicide.

In spite of consistent denials by the British Admiralty and the US embassy in Berlin that the *Ark Royal* had not been sunk, the German radio stations continued to ask questions about her whereabouts. Months afterwards, when the *Ark Royal* was in Rio de Janeiro, the ship's company sent Oberleutnant Francke an invitation to become an honorary member of their mess.

During the next two years the Germans and the Italians were to be in no doubt of the existence of the *Ark Royal*. The carrier's fighters were to shoot down or damage more than 100 enemy aircraft, and offer her great protection to many convoys in the Atlantic and Mediterranean. In addition, her torpedo-bombers were to wreak havoc on the aerodromes of Sardinia.

It would not be until 14 November 1941 that the German High Command could confidently report the loss of the *Ark Royal*. The previous day she had been steering towards Gibraltar in company with the *Malaya*, the *Argus*, the *Hermione* and seven destroyers. The weather was fair and the Force was in sight of the Rock. Twelve aircraft were flown off the carrier for a training exercise. Shortly before 4 p.m., when the last of the returning Swordfish was about to land, there was a tremendous explosion under the bridge of the carrier. The torpedo which caused the explosion was fired by the German submarine *U-81*. The loss of the *Ark Royal* was announced in London at one o'clock in the afternoon of 14 November. This time it was true. The Germans had sunk the *Ark Royal*.

5 · Sink the *Hood*

Following a Luftwaffe reconnaisance report that the battle cruiser HMS *Hood* was in the Firth of Forth estuary, nine of the new Junkers Ju 88 'Wonder' bombers of 1st Gruppe of KG 30 took off from their base at Westerland, Sylt shortly after 11 a.m. on 16 October. Led by Hauptmann Helmut Pohle, one of Junkers' top test pilots, the crews had strict orders to restrict their attacks to warships at sea. To their disappointment the raiders discovered that the *Hood* was berthed inside the Rosyth harbour and thus 'out of bounds' to them. Undaunted, Pohle and his men switched their attack to the smaller cruisers *Edinburgh* and *Southampton*, which were lying near the Forth Bridge and thus 'legitimate' targets. Singling out the *Southampton*, Pohle put his aircraft into a steep dive before releasing a 1,100 lb bomb. This crashed through the warship's starboard side but failed to explode.

Meanwhile, Spitfires of 602 (City of Glasgow) Squadron and 603 (City of Edinburgh) Squadron were scrambled only after the raiders had been sighted. It was rumoured later that the armoury at RAF Turnhouse had been locked, so delaying the supply of ammunition to the fighters. German intelligence mistakenly reported that there were no Spitfires based in Scotland. Furthermore, the British Radar Station's power was off, a stroke of luck for Pohle and his crew. Pohle's luck, however, was about to run out!

Helmut Pohle with the author (May 1992)

Pohle was now flying in a half-open aircraft. His canopy had been destroyed by naval fire. His plane was spotted off May Island, situated at the mouth of the Firth of Forth, by Flight Lieutenant George Pinkerton of 602 Squadron. Pinkerton waited for Pohle to emerge from cloud cover before swooping in for the kill. His Spitfire lurched as the cannon fire burst underneath, but the stricken raider eventually crashed into the sea off Crail, Fife.

Pohle was dragged from the sea by a Royal Navy destroyer but his crewmen were either dead or dying. Pohle collapsed on the deck of the destroyer with concussion and severe facial injuries. After spending a few days in the Royal Naval Hospital at Port Edgar, he was transferred to a military hospital in Edinburgh Castle. He later recalled:

> I remember being transported from the naval hospital to a little one-bed room ward in the castle. It looked like a kind of tower room with a little window in a niche. A private from the Scots Guards was seated by my bed armed with a rifle. One day I had a visit from Flight Lieutenant Pinkerton – the pilot who had shot me down. He brought me cigarettes and chocolates but I was unable to have a conversation with him.
>
> During the last week of November I was allowed to walk round the Castle under armed escort. Shortly before I was transferred from the Castle hospital I remember attending a concert. The Newhaven Fisherwives Choir was the main attraction and was well received by local British soldiers and POWs.

Pohle was transferred to the Tower of London on 2 December and, later, sent to No.1 Prisoner-of-War Camp at Grizedale Hall in the Lake District. Along with other captured Luftwaffe crews, he eventually ended up in a Canadian POW camp. Repatriated in 1947, he became a successful farmer in northern Germany.

Minutes after Pinkerton's success, Flight Lieutenant Pat Gifford of 603 Squadron was about to open his squadron's account. Oberleutnant Walter Storp, a veteran of the Spanish Civil War, was shot down by Gifford, and his aircraft fell into the sea four miles off Port Seaton. Storp, along with his crewmen Feldwebel Kohnke and Feldwebel Hielscher, were captured, uninjured, by a local trawler, *Dayspring*. The Ju 88 sank but was later recovered.

Although the *Edinburgh* and the *Southampton* had sustained only slight damage initially, the rest of the Ju 88s were more successful, inflicting heavier damage on the *Edinburgh* and the Tribal Class destroyer *Mohawk*. Naval gunner John Kerr was on board the *Mohawk* when the attack took place. He later recalled:

> I was doing my washing when the 'Action Stations' alarms sounded but we all thought that it was a trial run. Then they went off again. I dropped what I was doing and put on a pair of overalls and ran to my gun. I was joined by the captain of the gun crew, Petty Officer Halewood.
>
> We started to get our gun loaded then we heard a loud engine roar. I looked over to the other side of the gun turret (twin 4.7s) and saw a large bomb just about to strike the water off our starboard side, approximately 30 feet away. It exploded and almost immediately I felt a pain in my head and fell to the deck. At the same time a water barrel was severed and came down on top of me. Pilot Officer Halewood got me up and I saw he was hit too. We heard firing from our afterdeck and from our Pom-Poms with other ships joining in. Our ship was a shambles with bodies everywhere. I tried to attend to our Sick Bay Chief Dent but when I turned him over I saw he was dead. His back had been ripped open. We could not believe that this was happening to us because we were so near RAF Turnhouse.
>
> All of the injured were taken to Port Edgar hospital. I had shrapnel wounds to the head. At night I was wakened by the staff giving me an injection. The next day I was

moved to another ward and discharged a few days later, in time to attend the funerals of my mates at Rosyth Cemetery.

The *Mohawk* lost 17 men including their skipper, Commander Jolly. The dead German aircrew were buried with full military honours at Portobello Cemetery in Edinburgh. A few weeks later Flight Lieutenants Pinkerton and Gifford were awarded DFCs for their part in the Firth of Forth raid. On 17 October KG 30 was ordered to attack the huge base at Scapa Flow. This time the raiders only succeeded in locating the veteran battleship the *Iron Duke*.

Although some near-misses damaged her sides the vessel was later towed away and beached. Soon after the Firth of Forth raid the Admiralty ordered that the 'Big Ships' be moved to the safety of western Scotland.

6   First to fall on British soil

Lieutnant Rolf Niehoff saw the moorland stretch of the Scottish hillside race in to meet him. The last few metres of altitude fell away and he tensed himself for the crash. Both engines of the Heinkel He III bomber had been silenced as the plane slithered along the heather before finally coming to rest on the hilltop below.

The date was 28 October 1939 and the lone reconnaissance aircraft of Stab KG 26, which had taken off two and a half hours earlier from its base at Westerland, Sylt, had been forced down near the village of Humbie in East Lothian, after being intercepted by fighters of 602 (City of Glasgow) and 603 (City of Edinburgh) Squadrons. The inhabitants of the small village (population 600), some ten miles from Edinburgh, had witnessed the downfall of the first enemy aircraft to be brought down on the British mainland during the Second World War.

Niehoff being introduced to the former West German Chancellor, Willy Brandt

How Niehoff must have cursed his bad luck and the changing weather conditions on that historic Saturday morning. As observer and commander of the aircraft he had successfully plotted its course across the North Sea to the first target area on the Firth of Clyde. At the controls was Unteroffizier Kurt Lehmkuhl, accompanied by Gefreiter Bruno Reimann (wireless operator/air gunner) and Obergefreiter Gottlieb Kowalke (engineer/air gunner).

Recalling the traumatic moments when his aircraft had been outpaced by the Spitfires and Lehmkuhl in desperation had brilliantly swerved and zig-zagged, missing treetops only by inches, Niehoff said:

*Unteroffizier Kurt Lehmkuhl (7th from right)
pilot of the 'Humbie Heinkel'*

Our aim that morning was to look for the British navy in the borders of Firth of Forth and Firth of Clyde. Secondly I was ordered to give a weather report when crossing the coastline of Great Britain. This was because our aircraft was the only one over Britain that day. In addition to these two different tasks I switched on the aerial photographic camera during the whole flight over the British mainland. This I did because I wanted to give our photo platoon something to do and get experience in this job.

The main reason for our bad luck had been the weather. When we first crossed the coastline of Scotland there had been a very nice high closed cloud cover so we could fly beneath these clouds in order to be able to hide in the clouds if something should happen. But when we arrived at the Edinburgh area on our way back these clouds had nearly completely dissolved. There were only a few very thin clouds and not sufficient to hide us. It is well known that on an October morning, a cloudy October morning, like on that day it is not possible to know before nine or ten o'clock if the clouds will stay or will dissolve so we had to take this risk.

If we had not alarmed the British air defences by the transmission of our weather report it might have been possible to evade the Spitfires but because of these problems the Spitfires were already waiting for us when we were on our way back and arrived at the Edinburgh area.

The Spitfires were indeed waiting for the early-morning intruders and had laid on a reception committee. Both of the auxiliary squadrons had been scrambled to intercept raid X40. Puffs of ack-ack fire over the Tranent area alerted Red section of 602, led by Flying Officer Archie McKellar and accompanied by Pilot Officer Ferguson, to their quarry and very soon they latched on to the Nazi raider. McKellar's devastating bursts soon silenced Kowalke in the rear gun turret.

Meanwhile Red section of 603, led by Flight Lieutenant Pat Gifford, along with Pilot Officer Robertson and Pilot Officer Gilroy, joined in the chase over the desolate Scottish countryside. The combined firepower of the British fighters sealed the Heinkel's fate before it ploughed onto the hillside at Kidlaw Hill. In addition to Kowalke's death, Reimann had also perished, breaking his neck as the bomber pancaked to a halt in the hollow.

Niehoff further recalls:

When we were shot down at about 4,000 metres, very soon both engines were stopped and we had to go down. There was a small thin layer of clouds but just no use. They followed me. So we had to make a forced landing and the speed was too high so my pilot must slow down the plane. It was lucky for at that moment when the plane was just

Above: Top Battle of Britain fighter ace Archie McKellar (second right) who was credited with the destruction of the 'Humbie Heinkel'

Left: Kurt Lehmkuhl (right) with his brother Fritz prior to the outbreak of war

stalling there was a hill, so we pushed on the hill without moving one metre forward. Fortunately I did not fall forward as we crashed but my pilot was pushed through the shattered nose of the aircraft.

The British air defence only reacted after more than half an hour when we returned from the Glasgow area. I don't know why they took so long to locate us. Sometime later I found out that our aircraft had caused the first air raid alarm in Northern Ireland.

I really don't know if the anti-aircraft batteries did succeed in damaging our plane but at least once I heard a shell explode and this meant that there had been at least one dangerously near hit. Unfortunately our air gunners had no chance against the Spitfires with eight machine guns each. I'm not quite sure but I believe the air gunners were hit and died during the first or second attack when they had spent their bullets and were forced to reload their guns.

One of the witnesses to the dramatic events of the day was Mr John K. Irvine, of Long Newton Farm, Humbie, who arrived within minutes at the scene of the crash-landing. His detailed description of events was transmitted by the BBC later that evening:

I was filling up sacks of barley about a quarter past ten when I heard a noise like the hurling of a barrow. That's what I thought it was at first, but it went on and on and came nearer, and then I knew it was the noise of guns. Then we saw a big black machine with two engines coming over the trees from the north-west. There were four British machines with it. They were circling round and rattling bullets into the German hard as they could do it.

I thought we ought to take cover, there were women workers there, but curiosity brought us out again, while we were running in and while we were running out, so that we saw the German go over the houses, so low that it almost touched the chimneys. Then they all went out of sight up over the hill, and a few minutes later I saw our fighters going back, all four of them. They seemed to be finished with the job, so we ran up the hill to see what had happened.

Two of the crew were dead. I expect they would be the gunners, and they must have been shot before they came my length because I never saw them firing at our planes. The machine had scraped its tail over a dyke and came down on the moor on an even keel. One of the crew was not hurt at all. He was pulling out his mate. By the time we got up there he had him drawn out and lying on the ground.

We tried to talk to the unwounded man but he did not know what we were saying, although he spoke a little English. The wounded man said he wanted a drink but the doctor said he ought not to have one. He had two bullet wounds in the back.

The police took the wounded man away. Before he went he shook hands with his mate. We got a gate off one of the fences and carried the wounded man down to the road and waited there until the ambulance came for him.

Lehmkuhl was taken to hospital in Edinburgh.

Another witness to the events of the day was Alex Imrie, a retired airline pilot, who remembers:

A moorland shoot was arranged for that Saturday, and as one of the beaters I was employed to drive the game towards the gentlemens' guns for which I was to be paid the princely sum of five shillings, and to be given a lunch of a pork pie and a bottle of lemonade.

During the forenoon aeroplanes appeared with amazing suddenness, these were Spitfires and they all appeared to be diving and flirting their guns at Kidlaw Hill two miles to the east. They kept this up for a seemingly long time, and I remember that the sound of the guns firing did not really sound like what I thought a machine gun should sound like at all, it being more of a tearing noise.

A shepherd's son with us did not partake of the pie and lemonade lunch but went home for his food to his nearby cottage home. He arrived back early and out of breath with the news that a big German aeroplane had landed on Kidlaw Hill and that Jock Imrie (my father) had got a thermos flask and a can of tinned meat (bully beef) from it. We just could not wait until the end of the day, and when we were finally released from our duties and had been paid our respective five shillings, we departed at high speed on our bicycles for Kidlaw Farm.

There was considerable activity there (people and cars) for a country Scottish farmstead, and it was easy to find the way to the German aeroplane. We left the road, followed the cart truck, abandoned our bikes and started up the hillside through knee-high heather and heath. Soon we were upon it, a big grey Heinkel 111, lying on a slight incline in the ground with its nose pushed in and its back broken. Apart from about fifty civilians there were a number of RAF officers who were concentrated around and they were in the act of putting up a rope around the aeroplane to keep the more inquisitive away. Two incendiary bombs were removed from the aeroplane as we were there and moved some way from it, placed under the watchful eye of an armed airman.

Absolutely riddled with bullet holes, the machine was a light blue underneath, and had a lion in a shield marking on the side of the fuselage nose. The shorn-off right-hand tail plane had been collected and brought in from the dry stone dyke about 100 yards away that it had hit on landing. We stayed until dark, then were urged to move away by the guards.

At home I found that my father did not have a thermos flask or any canned meat, although at the time he could have 'collected' that sort of souvenir, but he wanted something with German writing on it and walked back to the severed tail plane to remove the maker's nameplate, breaking the blade of his penknife in the effort. He commented on how fresh and clean the observer looked, and also remarked that the dead gunners were carried down the hill side using five barred wooden crates as stretchers.

Most evenings after that weekend I would cycle up to Heinkel landing site and spend an hour or so chatting to the airmen on guard. I was allowed to sit in the pilot's seat, and I remember feeling the sharp edges of the aluminium around the bullet holes in the seat back and bottom that had wounded the pilot. After about a week only the forward section of the fuselage was left, then that too went, until there was only flattened heather and many little scraps of Perspex and grey and blue painted aluminium to show that there had ever been anything there.

Shortly after emerging from the bullet-ridden Heinkel, Niehoff set about the task of surveying the damage. By some miracle, he had managed to escape relatively unscathed, or so he thought at the time. Incredibly, the bomber had managed to remain fairly intact but the nose of the aircraft had been shattered on impact. His pilot had plummeted through the Perspex nose as he had battled the controls until the end. Lehmkuhl was alive and still grasping the control column. Niehoff was not sure if both his gunners had managed to survive but the eerie silence from within the wreckage seemed to confirm his worst fears.

The aircraft commander remembers being led away from the crash site by some policemen, who took him to the local police station. Later, a British Army captain arrived with his private car and drove him to a building which looked like the headquarters of a regimental organization. A colonel was there and they asked him for his name; Niehoff recalls him being 'very polite and gentlemanlike'. He was then taken to their officers' mess, where he had lunch together with a number of other officers. Very soon afterwards, he was transported to Edinburgh Castle, where he waited some time in the Guardroom. He was then escorted to some tower at the Castle, where he was detained for three or four hours.

Senior RAF officers asked him some questions. He remembers that he had the intention to 'stay upright' and 'put on a good show'. They asked him questions, including 'Who shot you down?', and further questioned him on the aircraft's engines. He told them that he knew everything about the engines but had no intention of telling them anything. It was clear that his interrogators had never seen the type of fuel that was in the Heinkel.

Later that afternoon, Niehoff was transported to London by train in the company of two soldiers with rifles. He was then locked up in the Tower of London for five days, an experience he describes as 'very nice and very comfortable'. Every morning a soldier would prepare a fire for him, and make his bed 'just like a hotel'. A sergeant from the military police later checked if the soldier had attended to all his daily chores. Niehoff later asked to see a doctor and he was sent for an examination to a hospital in Woolwich. Following an X-ray, it was discovered that he had broken his back when the plane had crash-landed.

The dead crewmen, Kowalke and Reimann, were buried in Edinburgh's Portobello Cemetery and accorded full military honours. Their remains were transferred to the German War Graves Cemetery at Cannock Chase, Staffordshire in 1959. Such an important event during the Phoney War inevitably led to propaganda outbursts from both British and German sources. The captured aircraft was dismantled and transported to the Royal Aircraft Establishment at Farnborough where it underwent stringent testing and examination.

The machine was one of the latest versions of its type, a Mark VA, with two Junkers Jumo 211A petrol-injection engines of 1,200 hp. Along with the Dornier Do 17s and Do 215s, the He IIIK shouldered most of the Luftwaffe's long-distance bombing and reconnaissance missions at that stage of the war. It was bigger than the Dornier and corresponded more to the British Vickers Wellington.

Following his stay in the Tower, Niehoff was sent to a POW camp for Luftwaffe officers at Grizedale Hall in the Lake District. He was later transported by ship from Bristol to a Canadian POW camp in the late summer of 1940. Further adventures were in store for him shortly after his arrival in Canada. Along with another Luftwaffe officer he was involved in the building of the first escape tunnel at a Canadian POW camp. Unfortunately for both the escape attempt was suddenly aborted when the tunnel very soon ended at a massive rock formation. Niehoff, along with his colleague, made history again as the first prisoners to be punished for an escape attempt.

The Bowmanville Camp band at their POW camp in Canada

A German POW orchestra at their camp in Canada

Rolf Niehoff, pictured in Germany (1988)   *The senior German officer (identity unknown) at Bowmanville POW camp in Canada*

He was repatriated to Germany in 1947 and very soon afterwards joined the new West German Air Force attaining the rank of Lieutenant Colonel before he retired in 1957. He now lives near Munich. After recovering from his injuries, Lehmkuhl also ended the war in a Canadian POW camp. He returned to his native Hamburg in 1947 and was employed with the German airline Lufthansa until his retirement. He died in 1984.

7   Fire over Whitby

Following reports that a British convoy was steering south of the north-east coast of England, No. 2 wing of KG 26 was ordered from their usual base in Westerland on 2 February. An offensive against British shipping in the North Sea was planned for first light on 3 February. For Feldwebel Hermann Wilms, the pilot of Heinkel No. 2323, and his crew of Unteroffiziers Peter Leushake (observer), Johann Meyer (flight engineer) and Karl Missy (air gunner) they were destined to occupy a unique place in the air war before the day had ended.

As usual in such anti-shipping actions, the crews were ordered to take off in pairs at three-minute intervals and steer west. After almost three hours' flying time, one of the aircraft should intercept the convoy. On locating the target, the others would commence the attack.

Minutes before Heinkel No. 2323 was approaching the Yorkshire coastline, the telephone rang in 43 Squadron's pilots' room at RAF Acklington, near Newcastle, 'Blue Section Scramble'. Within a short time three Hurricanes took off into the frosty morning air. Leading the trio was flight Lieutenant Peter Townsend with 'Tiger' Folkes and Sergeant Hallowes following in his wake. 'SECTOR 180, BANDIT ATTACKING SHIPPING OFF WHITBY, BUSTER.'

Describing the historic action in his book, *Duel of Eagles*, Group Captain Townsend recalls:

> We raced south at full throttle, a few feet above the waves, to have the best chance of intercepting them.
>
> '*Achtung, Jaeger!*' Suddenly Peter Leushake saw three fighters curving up steeply from below. The words were hardly past his lips when bullets ripped into the Heinkel and killed him. At the same instant, in the lower gun position, Meyer, the flight engineer, was badly wounded. Only Missy, in the top rear gun position, remained to defend the stricken aircraft. He aimed carefully and fired at the leading Hurricane. His single MG 15 was a feeble answer to the eight .303 Brownings of the British fighter, which was firing again. Missy never moved from his swivel seat at the gun position. He knew the fighter's second volley had hit him, but he could not tell how badly.
>
> Hermann Wilms pulled the Heinkel up into the cloud layer just above, but the speed dropped off sharply until the bomber sagged in his hands and he knew the engines were hit. It was a mile or two to the coast, but somehow Wilms made it, gliding over Whitby town.

Eventually, after flying low over houses in the Castle Park area of the town, the raider came down in a field on Bannial Flat Farm. Its impetus carried it across the field in the direction of two cottages, at the entrance of the approach to Mr P. A. Smales' house. Crashing through a hedge it struck a tree, snapping it off by the stump as though it were a twig; and this impact caused the plane to swerve to the right and miss hitting the cottages by a few feet.

Telephone wires were cut as the Heinkel neared the spot where it came to rest. Mrs Smales and Miss A. M. Sanderson were among those early on the scene, and Meyer and Missy were carried in to the house. Tea was made for them and they were supplied with cigarettes. Wilms, Missy and Meyer were taken to Whitby Hospital where Meyer died from his injuries later that day.

The *Whitby Gazette* also reported that two Heinkels had been sighted off the Yorkshire coast machine gunning a trawler, killing the Captain and injuring two of the crew.

Special Constable Arthur Barratt dashed up to the burning Heinkel just in time to see Wilms burning the aircrafts papers. It took five fire extinguishers and shovels full of snow to put the fire out. Meyer was screaming in agony while Missy had been grievously wounded with one leg broken and the other terribly mutilated. Missy's right leg was later amputated.

Leushake and Meyer were later buried by 43 Squadron at Catterick. On their wreath was a simple message, 'From 43 Squadron, with sympathy.'

Due to the extent of his injuries, Missy was returned to Germany in exchange for Allied prisoners of war in October 1943.

Heinkel No. 2323 was the first enemy plane to crash on English soil during the Second World War, the RAF's previous similar success having been in Scotland in October 1939.

8   The Suicide Gang

Sandy Wood, skipper of the trawler *Star of the Isles*, revelled in the beauty of the bright but frosty February morning. He could feel the change of movement in the boat as it passed from the tranquil waters of the harbour to the open sea. Sandy blew a blast on the siren, and a woman at the quayside waved back. 'We're celebrating our 16th wedding anniversary,' he said proudly. In the distance he could see the two other Granton boats, *Star of the East* and *Starbank*. The three 'Star' trawlers had been brought north from Scarborough six years earlier to fish out of Granton and Leith in the Firth of Forth. Their main fishing grounds were 150 miles from the Scottish coastline, and lay in the direct path of the Luftwaffe's crack reconnaissance squadrons KG 26 and KG 30, based on the Frisian island of Sylt.

During the early days of the conflict the Luftwaffe crews had mainly confined themselves to reconnaissance and the laying of magnetic mines. Although many fishing boats had reported sightings of German aircraft and seaplanes there were relatively few hostile incidents, but at the beginning of 1940 the Luftwaffe High Command changed their strategy. It seemed now that almost anything that moved in British territorial waters was to be considered 'fair game'. Throughout January and February the British east-coast fishing fleet was being bombed and machine gunned almost every time they went about their business. Many of the attacks were delivered from heights of less than 200 feet. The 'Star' vessels along with others formed a part of what became known as 'The Suicide Gang'. Each trawler carried a twin Lewis machine gun in its stern, the only defence against air attacks.

The 'baby' of the *Star of the Isles* crew was Robert 'Blondie' Lonie, a local lad who came from a long line of Leith seafarers. The youngster was already a seasoned war veteran, having spent three days adrift in an open boat when his first ship, the *Astros*, was bombed and strafed by enemy aircraft. Robert, along with three other members of the crew, eventually managed to take to the ship's lifeboat. Three hours later they were rescued by a Royal Navy minesweeper. Making his second trip on that February morning, and four days out of port, Robert was taking his turn at the wheel. As dawn broke he heard the drone of aircraft engines, searched the sky through his binoculars, saw the plane with its distinctive swastika markings. 'German plane! German plane!' His frantic cries brought the rest of the crew running up the companionway.

Two of them dashed to the gun. Skipper Wood ran to the bridge and shook his fist at the German raider. 'You bloody swine!' he roared. 'You'll no dae me oot o' ma wedding anniversary.' Wood raced to his cabin and snatched up the radio telephone: 'Wick Radio…Wick Radio…

we're being attacked by a German bomber.' Before he had time to finish his message, machine gun fire ripped through the funnel, and bullets ricochetted off the decks. Then the trawlers hit back. Bob Liston, on the *Star of the Isles*, swung his Lewis gun into action and let fly with a stream of bullets skywards.

Flashes of flame from the *Star of the East* and *Starbank* confirmed that all the ships' gunners were in action. As the German raiders swooped on their third attack great explosions shook the sea as the plane released aerial torpedoes. All failed to find their target. By now the Heinkel had been caught in the intense crossfire. The plane vanished with a cloud of smoke trailing from its engine. Sandy Wood brought his boat and his crew safely home and celebrated his 16th wedding anniversary.

Although a number of trawlers were sunk by German U-boats during the first few weeks of the war, the air attacks and involvement of fishing boats really hit the headlines on 16 October when nine Junkers 88s of KG 30 attacked shipping in the Firth of Forth. Following attacks by Spitfires of 603 Squadron one of the bombers plunged into the sea three miles north of Port Seaton. The skipper of the local trawler *Dayspring*, John Dickson, along with his two sons John and William, headed towards the downed raider. Although the aircraft stayed afloat for a while, by the time the trawler arrived on the scene, only three of the crew, including the pilot, were alive. The pilot, Oberleutnant Sigmund Storp, gave his signet ring to the trawler skipper and thanked him for saving his life.

The hit-and-run tactics were stepped up after the 16 October raid with Scottish fishing vessels sustaining some heavy losses. On 17 December three trawlers fell victim to German aircraft off the Isle of May, near Fife Ness. The *Compaganus*, along with the *Isabella Greig* and the *Trinity NB* were all Leith-based boats. All three trawlers were sunk. Injured crew members from the *Isabella Greig* were landed at Granton and taken to Leith hospital. Earlier nine members of the crew of the *Compaganus* were landed at Aberdeen.

The air raids and harrassment of the small boats continued into the New Year, and on 12 January the Scarborough trawler *Persian Empire* came under attack from a Heinkel. After unloading four bombs, the raider circled around the trawler and released four more. This was accompanied by machine gun fire but the 195-ton vessel somehow escaped serious damage, before limping back to port. Trawlers off Bridlington were also attacked on 12 January. However, on this occasion, the Heinkel raider was driven off by anti-aircraft guns on the ships.

The attacks on vessels off the Yorkshire coast continued with the Grimsby trawler *Rose of England* and the Glasgow collier *Yewdale* being targeted on 3 February. Two Heinkels attacked the vessels, both of which were severely damaged and towed into the safety of Scarborough harbour. The captain of the *Yewdale* died from his injuries, and two of his crew were wounded in the attack. No-one was hurt aboard the trawler but skipper Charlie Bruce reported that the ship had been hit three times by bomb shrapnel and by many bullets. Two enemy planes, possibly the same ones, were shot down later that day; one near Whitby and one off the Tyne. Also attacked and damaged that day was the 225-ton trawler *Nairana*, fishing at the time in Bridlington Bay.

Six days later an air raid was directed at the 276-ton North Shields trawler *Lowdock*, fishing in company with another trawler off Scarborough. Close by were three Scarborough cobles *Hilda*, *BS Colling* and *Our Maggie*, and they, too, came under attack, causing them to abandon their lines and head for the safety of the harbour. Skipper Harry Sheader, of the *Hilda*, counted 30 bombs dropped altogether along with machine gun fire but the small boats all escaped unscathed.

The Scarborough keelboat *Courage* was in the vicinity too, and though she did not come under fire on this occasion she was bombed and machine gunned while lying off Whitby about the same time, though the raiders scored no direct hits. One bomb landed so close that it split the vessel's exhaust pipe, and crewman Ernie Kitto, who had been below at the time, emerged from the engine-room covered in soot and water. No-one was hurt, however, and the *Courage* sailed into safety at Whitby.

It was reported in the House of Commons on 14 February that the arming of trawlers would be given top priority. Replying to Mannie Shinwell, who asked whether he hoped that within a month or six weeks every vessel trading in the North Sea would be protected with guns, Winston Churchill replied: 'Yes, sir. I have every hope that a very great measure of protection will be afforded to our men in this dangerous area. It appears that every vessel must be effectively armed to resist murderous attacks.'

Less than three weeks later, Grand Admiral Erich Raeder, Commander in Chief of the German navy, speaking on American radio, claimed that British fishing vessels were being used as naval auxiliaries and therefore could be treated as any other hostile ship. By the end of March many trawlers had been equipped with anti-aircraft guns, usually Lewis guns, and their crews had received gunnery training. The quality of the training was open to question as there were many recorded instances of guns jamming or failing to work when they were most needed. To add to that, the training sessions usually amounted to no more than a couple of hours.

9 Rudolf Behnisch and his 'second birthday'

In the first week of April 1940, the Luftwaffe crews were still under strict orders not to fly over the British mainland. Seven months had elapsed since that fateful September morning when, only half an hour after Chamberlain's declaration of war, the air raid sirens had sent people to cover for the first time. Apart from the 16 October raid in the Firth of Forth, Goering's airmen had mainly concentrated on 'hit-and-run' tactics against convoys within British coastal waters. During the early months of 1940 harassment of east-coast shipping was a common practice.

At Lübeck-Blankensee in northern Germany, Oberstleutnant Hans Hefele, heading Second Group KG 26, had some unexpected news for his pilots. Today, Wednesday 3 April, he would fly as an additional gunner on a sortie against British convoys. He wanted to see for himself how things were going on these missions. Leutnant Rudolf Behnisch, a tall fair-haired Reservist with an infectious sense of humour, was chosen to pilot the Gruppenkommandeur's Heinkel 1H+AC on an armed reconnaissance against the British convoys. Hefele's Second Group aircraft were to operate in pairs along the British east coast. The plan called for a low cloud base with the raiders simultaneously pressing home their attacks at different points along the coast.

That same morning, the Scarborough drifter *Silver Line* was on her way to her fishing grounds, unaware of the drama that was to unfold later that day. Three weeks earlier the skipper, Bill Watkinson, and his crew had been bombed by a German plane but had escaped unharmed. It was 12.20 p.m. when Flight Lieutenant Norman Ryder of 41 Squadron, based at West Hartlepool, was scrambled to investigate a raider in the Whitby area. Using his call sign of Red One, Ryder was vectored across the coast at Staithes in Spitfire N.3114. Hefele and his crew were already in trouble when Ryder spotted them. Down to 400 feet, the Heinkel was fighting for survival on its port engine, after receiving a number of direct hits from Royal Naval gunners.

Sensing that the big bomber was in trouble, Ryder swooped in for the kill, firing at the Heinkel's starboard engine from 400 yards astern. After firing a second burst from within 200 yards without any noticeable effect, Red One was jostled by slipstream as he broke away to port. Hefele, crouching in the front turret, opened fire at the Spitfire. The 'additional' gunner found his target with concentrated bursts. Smoke streaming from his engine, Ryder's aircraft lost power suddenly before crashing into the sea. The aircraft was sinking rapidly before Ryder struggled free. However, help was close at hand. Hauled aboard the Grimsby trawler *Alaska*,

The Scarborough drifter Silver Line

Norman Ryder (seated centre) with fellow pilots, North Weald (1941)

Flt Lieutenant Norman Ryder (left). His was the first Spitfire to be shot
down by the Luftwaffe and the first pilot to ditch a Spitfire

The Silver Line *crew with Tom Watkinson manning the machine gun*

Behnisch and crew prior to the Scarborough raid

Ryder spent a wet, miserable afternoon drying out in the boiler room, before he was landed safely at Hartlepool.

The crew of the *Silver Line* were hauling in their nets when the crippled Heinkel swooped down towards them. Fortunately, the aircraft was some distance away, giving Tom Watkinson enough time to swing the Lewis gun into action. Waiting until the aircraft was well within his range, Tom let loose at the raider. A stream of tracer fire found its target and the stricken Heinkel swerved wildly and plunged into the sea. Behnisch succeeded in what he described later as a 'tail-landing' in the seven-foot-high waves. Jubilant at their their 'kill', skipper Watkinson, along with his brothers Bob and Tom, watched anxiously as the Luftwaffe crew scrambled clear of the sinking Heinkel. The drifter drew alongside and prepared to rescue the ditched flyers.

Behnisch recalled:

> Two of my five-man crew tried to get our rubber dinghy afloat, but it was punctured all over by bullets and submerged right away. We all went into the water as the Heinkel sank more and more. I then realised that my life vest did not hold the air, so I climbed back onto the tail still above the water while the fuselage was already submerged.
>
> We swam over to the approaching boat and the crew lowered ropes. We managed to haul ourselves aboard and lay down. We were invited to drink from a bottle of whisky while one man covered us with a shotgun. I handed my gold signet ring to one of the fishermen and thanked him for saving my life.
>
> I found out later that his name was Tom Watkinson. I have always regarded 3 April 1940 as my second birthday. We were escorted below where we got rid of our wet overalls, uniforms and underwear, rubbed ourselves down with warm towels and put on clean underwear, trousers and heavy pullovers. I remember there was some joking about my big feet, so they managed to procure some fitting rubber boots in which I travelled, first class, to London next day. All of us were landed at Scarborough harbour early that evening. Our wounded navigator was transported to a hospital where, as he told me later, his rescuers visited him after some days, presenting him with gifts of oranges, sweets and cigarettes. We remaining four were taken to the local police station in the harbour area and separated.
>
> Following interrogation by a senior RAF intelligence officer I was transported in a car to a villa which served as an officers' mess for an artillery unit. Later a young officer asked whether I would like some music and brought some records. I chose the song – 'I am an Optimist' – and everyone laughed in a quiet relaxed atmosphere.

The Heinkel crew were sent to a prisoner-of-war camp in England before they were transported to another camp in Canada. All of them made a safe return to Germany several years later. Rudolf Behnisch was released from captivity on 16 March 1947. Classified as a 'fugitive from the East', his lost homeland being Silesia, he studied languages at the University of Hamburg. He became a civil servant in 1948 and in 1953 moved with his federal office to Wiesbaden. He has two daughters and retired in 1976.

A few days after the North Sea drama, the *Silver Line* crew was received at Scarborough town hall by the mayor. The fishermen were presented with silver statuettes of lifeboatmen for their heroic efforts. A message to the skipper on behalf of the Scarborough Corporation read, 'We have all been thrilled to hear of the part which you and your crew played in helping

Above: The Anglo Saxon *lifeboat*

Left: A member of the Watkinson family with the statuette presented to his father in recognition of rescuing Behnisch and his crew in 1940

Below: Silver Line *crew with the statuette presented by Scarborough Borough Council*

Luftwaffe pilot Rudolph Behnisch whose crippled Heinkel was forced to ditch after attacking shipping off the Yorkshire coast

Behnisch with the author (May 1992)

Rudolph Behnisch (centre) with fellow prisoners in Canada

bring down a German plane and rescuing the crew.' Flight Lieutenant Norman Ryder had the dubious honour of achieving two 'firsts' in rapid succession. His was the first Spitfire to be shot down by the Luftwaffe and he was the first pilot to ditch a Spitfire. Awarded the DFC for his North Sea exploits, Ryder went on to distinguish himself in the Battle of Britain. He retired from the RAF as a Group Captain in 1960.

10 The Moray Firth raid

It was General Hans Ferdinand Geisler's 10th Air Corps, which included KG 26, equipped with the Heinkel III, and KG 30, equipped with the fast, up-to-date Ju 88s, that had spearheaded the early attacks on British shipping around the British coastline. Geisler's squadrons were heavily committed to daylight missions, known as 'armed reconnaissance' over mainland Scotland, Orkney and Shetland. For more than six months Geisler's crews had conducted a series of well co-ordinated and systematic attacks on British naval units along the north-east coastline from Yorkshire to Orkney and Shetland. On 9 April Hitler gave the green light for the invasion of Norway and Denmark. The Luftwaffe objectives were now to be directed at the Norway theatre and so the raids over the British coastline were drastically cut back.

The following day Ober-leutnant Harald Vogel, a tall, lean Bavarian, along with his four man crew in a Heinkel III of 4/KG 26, were preparing for one of the last attacks in British coastal waters during that stage of the Phoney War. Their target was to be a convoy in the Moray Firth area. It was the 20-year-old pilot's first operational flight and proved to be a true baptism of fire. Pressing home his attacks from a height of 18,000 feet, where no naval

Rudolph Behnisch (left) along with Harold Vogel (right) at their POW camp in Canada

guns could reach him, Vogel's aircraft was set upon by five Hurricanes of 603 (City of Edinburgh) and 605 (County of Warwick) Squadrons. The Hurricanes' combined fire-power of 40 .303 Browning machine guns proved too much for Vogel's aircraft as it plunged into the sea some ten miles off Kinnaird Head, near Fraserburgh. Although 603 Squadron had already achieved some spectacular victories in the early days of the conflict, for the 605 fliers it was their first real taste of success. Describing the dramatic events of that spring morning, Vogel recalled:

> Of the crew of four, two other ranks (a mechanic-gunner and a wireless operator-gunner) were shot during the first stages of the attack. The observer (who had been promoted to corporal that very day) and I left the plane by parachutes after both engines had caught fire. I was the only one to survive and was picked out of the water by the British destroyer *Ulster* which had escorted the convoy under attack.
>
> As far as I could ascertain later, the destroyer was part of the navy reserve immobilised in peace time and re-activated for the war. As I was slightly wounded, the medical staff aboard took care of my wounds and placed me in a hammock. Then the commander of the vessel paid me a formal visit, regretted that we were at war as he had some good friends in Germany, and left a package of Players cigarettes with me.
>
> About 24 hours later the *Ulster* disembarked me at the Royal Navy installations at the shore of the Firth of Forth opposite Edinburgh city, and an ambulance brought me to the military hospital in the castle. I was accommodated in a small one-bed room containing a small window, left open, within the mighty walls of the castle. From that instant on I was guarded by an Army soldier sitting beside my bed day and night. I remember especially one, a Scotchman, apparently drafted for the daylight shift, with whom I tried to maintain conversation as good as my very poor knowledge of the English language allowed it.
>
> In civilian life he was a coalminer, and he gave me a very interesting account of the normal manner of living of his family and of Scottish coalminers generally. Of the many hours of conversation I had with him, two features prevail in my memory – his deep devotion to the Royal Family and his acceptance of the social system apparently prevailing in Scotland at that time, with high class people and low class people existing by the will of God. But one thing he resented very much – that he was forced to stand to attention each time a Sister entered the room. Needless to say that we could not agree in our conversations, in spite of the friendly manner in which they were maintained, on the reasons for the outbreak for the war and on the chances to win it.
>
> As far as I remember, I arrived at the hospital on a Wednesday. A surgeon inspected the bandages on my wounds as applied at the *Ulster*, and found them OK. I was a little puzzled that he preferred not to change them, including one at my right shoulder where, apparently, a bullet was stuck.

The following Saturday Vogel found that his right arm was swollen and painful and that it had assumed a dark colour. He indicated to a nurse that he thought his arm required immediate attention. The nurse's first reaction was that he could not expect such special attention during a weekend. In desperation the wounded pilot persuaded her to alert another member of the hospital staff, who took a further look at his injured arm concluding that the injury was indeed very bad. A few minutes later Vogel was strapped to a stretcher and carried up a narrow spiral staircase into another ward to await an operation.

Vogel further recalled:

> A surgeon informed me that he had to narcotise me for an operation. Upon my request he assured me that he would not amputate my arm. Within a few days after the operation my condition improved considerably under the kind care of the nurses. Later the Sister

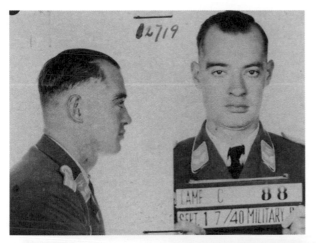

Left: Vogel with his ID 'mug shot'

Below: George Pinkerton displaying the map where Pohle's aircraft plunged into the sea

and the surgeon even prescribed a bottle of stout daily to me. Jokingly he said that he could not prescribe a bottle of Lowenbrau. Continuing in this friendly atmosphere he told me that he had spent some of his student days in Munich where he had acquired a knowledge of German. One of the nurses even bought from her own funds a small English/German pocket dictionary which she donated to me.

My room was close to a fairly large sick-room with, perhaps, 20 beds where a German non-commissioned officer was accommodated among British forces personnel. I was not allowed, however, to establish contact with him, although I could see him one day when I could attend a concert given in the large room for the entertainment of the patients. Probably he was a member of the crew of Hauptmann Pohle who had been shot down while attacking a British cruiser in the Firth of Forth with a Ju 88 dive-bomber, thereby flying under the famous bridge. He was much more seriously wounded than I and had spent a long time in the hospital before I had arrived. Later I met Pohle in officers' POW camps in England and Canada, but have not heard of him for more than 40 years.

Luftwaffe bomber crews prior to an attack on the British coastline from their base at Lubeck Blankensee

I was also pleased to meet a British naval officer sometimes during the morning toilet in the lavatory of the hospital. Unfortunately, I cannot remember his name but he spoke fluent German and said that he had done a lot of travelling in Germany for 'observation'. He claimed to have been a member of the Runciman Committee which had investigated the situation in the Sudeten area of Czechoslovakia in 1938 and had (as far as I can remember), recommended the handing over of that area to Hitler's Germany, as later decided at the Munich Conference.

Three weeks later Vogel was discharged from the castle hospital and transferred to the famous 'London Cage' interrogation centre at Cockfosters in north London. Vogel was questioned there over a one-week period and it was there he made his first contact with other imprisoned German officers. Along with other captured Luftwaffe crews he was sent to the then No. 1 Officers' POW camp at Grizedale Hall near Lake Windermere. In June 1940 he was transferred by sea from Liverpool to Montreal, and for the next six years he was interned in various camps in Ontario and Alberta, before being returned to Britain in 1946. He was discharged from captivity on 23 November 1946.

Vogel continued:

Today I am looking back with gratitude on the fair treatment in Great Britain, Canada and especially at the castle in Edinburgh. My sojourn there was not yet over-shadowed by the extreme hatred developed during the later stages of the war or by the knowledge of incredible atrocities committed later by German personnel especially in Eastern Europe. No German bomb had fallen at that time on British soil, as far as I know, except perhaps for some attacks on navy installations at Scapa Flow.

The above recollections were conveyed in a letter to the Scottish United Services Museum at Edinburgh Castle in late November 1986. After the war ended, Vogel spent six years with the Joint Export/Import Agency, established by the British and United States military governments in the then West Germany for the revival of German trade. Later he was employed by the British and US High Commissions. Like many other former Second World War Luftwaffe personnel, Vogel later enlisted in the West German Air Force. He attained the rank of major, and recalled, with a certain amount of humour, that he became a member of the RAF officers mess at 2nd Allied Tactical Air Force HQ at Mönchengladbach. Following his retirement from the Air Force he served for ten years as a commercial officer with the Canadian Consulate General in Düsseldorf.

11   Scotland the brave

In the very early stages of the Second World War Scotland and its civilians witnessed a number of air war 'firsts': the first German bomber shot down, the first bombs on British soil, and the first civilians killed by an enemy bomb. In a sense the battle for control over the skies of Orkney, as the Luftwaffe sought to destroy the Home Fleet anchored in Scapa Flow, was decided long before the Battle of Britain began. Scotland-based Coastal Command units were also in the thick of the action from the beginning of the conflict.

Formed as a light bomber squadron of the Auxiliary Air Force at Turnhouse, near Edinburgh, on 14 October 1925, 603 (City of Edinburgh) Squadron was equipped initially with DH 9As. The following years saw the consolidation of the squadron into an effective flying unit operating Westland Wapiti IIAs and Hawker Harts. The year 1938 was memorable for the squadron's conversion to a fighter squadron on 24 October, operating Hawker Hinds and Gloster Gladiator Mk Is. It also won the coveted Esher Trophy awarded annually to the premier auxiliary squadron. On 16 October 1939 Spitfires of 602 (City of Glasgow) and 603 squadrons engaged nine Junkers Ju 88s of KG 30, based at Westerland, which were attacking shipping in the Firth of Forth. For the first time the Spitfire was to go into action against the enemy. Two of the German aircraft were shot down, the first being credited by Fighter Command to Flight Lieutenant Pat Gifford of Red Section 603 Squadron (consisting of Spitfires L1070 XT-A (Flight Lieutenant Gifford), L1050 (Pilot Officer Robertson) and L1061 XT-B (Flying Officer H. MacDonald), and the second to Flight Lieutenant G. C. Pinkerton of 602 Squadron.

On 28 October the Spitfires of both 603 and 602 Squadrons shared in the destruction of a Heinkel He III-H of Stabsstaffel KG 26 based at Lübeck-Blankensee, which was brought down close to the village of Humbie, near Dalkeith in Midlothian. This was the first German aircraft to crash on British soil, both aircraft shot down on 16 October having fallen in the sea off Port Seaton. Both Flight Lieutenants Pinkerton and Gifford were awarded DFCs for these actions.

From this period onwards 603 Squadron was always at the forefront of any operational activity. First it moved to Hornchurch in August 1940 to play its part in the Battle of Britain, moving back to Drem in December. A return to Hornchurch was made in May 1941, where the squadron took part in cross-channel sweeps and bomber escort duties. By the end of this period 603 Squadron had been credited with 171 enemy aircraft destroyed and over 200

Flight Lieutenant Pinkerton (second from left) at readiness with fellow fighter pilots

The 'Humbie' Heinkel

The 'Humbie' Heinkel soon after crash landing

Onlookers gather around the crash site

probably destroyed or damaged. It was during this period Pilot Officer Richard Hillary, author of *The Last Enemy*, served with 603 Squadron.

Richard Hillary was shot down in flames over the English Channel on 3 September 1940, flying Spitfire X4277 XT-M. He was shot down by Hauptmann Bode of II/JG 26 during a combat off Margate. Hillary baled out. He was grievously burnt but was rescued by Margate lifeboat and admitted to hospital. He eventually recovered and returned to flying duties. Just after midnight on 8 January 1943 Blenheim BA194 crashed and burst into flames near the village of Duns, Berwickshire, killing Flight Lieutenant Richard Hope Hillary, RAFVR, and his navigator, Walter Fison. At nightfighter OTUs this was not an uncommon event, which caused the nickname of Slaughterhall to be given to Charterhall.

After a short period at Dyce, Aberdeen, 603 Squadron embarked for Malta on the carrier USS *Wasp*, being committed to the island's defence from April 1942. In three months of intensive air fighting over 60 enemy aircraft destroyed and a further 60 probably destroyed or damaged had been added to the squadron's scoreboard. In August 1942 the aircraft and aircrew were absorbed into 229 Squadron at Ta' Qali, Malta.

On 1 February 1943 the squadron was reformed as a strike unit in the Middle East equipped with Beaufighter Mks I, VI and X which it operated successfully from North Africa on anti-shipping strikes in the Mediterranean and Aegean. During this time 603 pioneered the use of rocket projectiles in this theatre of war. In December 1944, by which time operations ceased prior to the return to the UK, over 50 vessels of various types had been sunk. During the latter part of this period the squadron was commanded by Wing Commander Christopher Foxley-Norris, who later became Air Chief Marshal Sir Christopher Foxley-Norris, GCB, DSO, OBE, MA, CBIM, FRSA.

Spitfire Mk XVs were issued to the unit on 7 January 1945, at Coltishall, Norfolk, and 603 Squadron was soon engaged in escorting Beaufighters on anti-shipping strikes and on separate fighter-bomber sorties against the new V2 rocket launch sites in Holland. With the end of the war in Europe, the squadron returned to its home base at Turnhouse, where it disbanded in August 1945. No. 603 Squadron finished the war with a formidable list of achievements:

Aircraft destroyed: confirmed 250, probable 121.3, damaged 167

Shipping destroyed: confirmed 50 (7,845 tons), probable 6 (8,004 tons), damaged: 6 (10,992 tons)

During the 1939–1945 war 603 Squadron was awarded 15 DFCs and 5 DFMs.

The squadron's battle honours include:

Home Defence 1940–42, Battle of Britain 1940, Channel and North Sea 1941, Fortress Europe 1942, Malta 1942, Mediterranean 1943, Sicily 1943, south-east Europe 1944.

No. 602 (City of Glasgow) Squadron was the first of 21 auxiliary squadrons to be formed within the Royal Air Force. It began flying from Moorpark Aerodrome at Renfrew. It was originally a bomber squadron but converted to fighters in May 1939. Two of its pilots, the Marquis of Douglas & Clydesdale (later the Duke of Hamilton), and Flight Lieutenant David McIntyre, were the first men to fly over Mount Everest. Such was the confidence of the Air Ministry in this unit that 602 was the first auxiliary squadron to be equipped with Spitfires and, indeed, seventh in the whole Royal Air Force. With these Spitfires it was involved in the shooting down of the first German aircraft in UK skies in the Second World War.

Later the squadron moved south into the thick of the Battle of Britain, where it soon established itself as one of the leaders, finishing the conflict with the second-highest total of 'kills' and the lowest pilot loss rate, and as the longest-serving squadron in the front line. The roll of honour displayed in the squadron's museum records this momentous time in our nation's history. After a spell at Prestwick and Ayr in early 1941, 602 Squadron returned south, flying strike sorties into Europe from Kenley and Redhill and later provided fighter cover during the Dieppe Raid in August 1942.

In September the squadron moved north to the Orkney and Shetland Islands to intercept the high-level German reconnaissance raiders over Scapa Flow. It flew from bases in the south of England from January 1943 and transferred to the Second Tactical Air Force in November, flying offensive sweeps over France and providing fighter escorts. Involved in the D-Day invasion, 602 later flew from airfields in Europe before returning to England in September 1944 to concentrate on strikes against V2 rocket sites and other prime targets. The squadron disbanded on 15 May 1945, by which time it was credited with the destruction of 150 enemy aircraft.

The first months of the air war over Scotland were almost entirely confined to armed reconnaisance, anti-shipping and mine-laying missions, often by individual aircraft but with some notable exceptions. The early rule that no land targets should be attacked applied even to ships in port, so any shipping had to be at sea before being attacked. There was, of course, a lot of shipping activity round the coasts of Britain, including the east coast of Scotland, with naval bases like Scapa Flow, Invergordon and Rosyth playing an important role, and convoys plying regularly between ports like Aberdeen, Dundee, Methil, Burntisland, Grangemouth and Leith, and others all round the coast.

The attacking aircraft at the outset of the war were mainly Heinkel He IIIs of the 'Lion' Bomber Group 26 and Junkers Ju 88s of the 'Eagle' Bomber Group 30 (KG 26 and KG 30 respectively). Their crews had been specially selected from different bomber units of the Luftwaffe.

They operated from their advance base, the airfield at Westerland, Sylt, the nearest part of Germany to Scotland. It was approximately 425 miles from Westerland to Fife Ness and Aberdeen, the round trip lasting at least four and a half hours for Junkers, and five and a half hours for Heinkels, depending on weather conditions and on time taken for attacks and/or evasion of pursuing fighters. There were also mine-laying Dorniers and Heinkel 115 floatplanes, the latter occasionally seen from the East Fife coast on the waters of the Firth of Forth, especially on moonlit nights.

Individual sporadic raids took place right up to April 1940 when the invasion and occupation of Denmark and Norway, starting on 9 April, changed the situation dramatically. Now air bases at Aalborg in northern Denmark for KG 30s Ju 88s and at Stavanger in Norway for the Heinkel IIIs of KG 26 brought them within easier reach of the Scottish coast. Stavanger to Fife Ness was about 365 miles, and Peterhead was just under 300 miles away. The saving in flying time averaged about one hour. Air activity over and near the east coast increased accordingly. German aircraft losses over and near Scotland for the first year of the war were, in fact, considerable, totalling approximately 50 by September 1940. Air attacks by individual aircraft and by small groups of aircraft continued during the remaining months of 1940 and the first few months of 1941. During this time London and other major cities were being blitzed, first of all by day, then mainly at night. Scotland's turn came on 13/14/15 March and 7/8 April and 5/6/7 May when Glasgow and Clydeside were heavily bombed. In these attacks approximately 1,000 tonnes of high-explosive and incendiary bombs were dropped and about 1,000 bombers were involved.

By the end of May 1941 Hitler had finalized his plans to attack Russia and every available bomber was being transferred to the Eastern front. By mid-June 1941 only about 300 bombers remained in the West, including those primarily involved in anti-shipping activities. Relatively few bombers were left behind in Norway and the result was that the latter half of the war was comparatively quiet in Scotland, as far as German bombing was concerned. There were, however, a few notable exceptions with Aberdeen having a short but sharp raid from 30 Dornier bombers in April 1943, when 91 people were killed.

German losses for the second year of the war, up to and including August 1941, totalled almost the same as for the first year, namely about 50, over or near Scotland. Enemy air activity continued on a considerable scale, although not necessarily resulting in the dropping of bombs.

The Heinkel III bombers of Bomber Group 26 were organized as follows:

[KAMPFGESCHWADER 26 (Bomber Group 26)]
{GESCHWADER STAB (Group HQ Staff Flight)}

1 GRUPPE (1 Wing)	11 GRUPPE (2 Wing)
STAB (1st Wing HQ Staff Flight)	STAB (2nd Wing HQ Staff Flight)
1 Staffel (No. 1 Squadron)	4 Staffel (No. 4 Squadron)
2 Staffel (No. 2 Squadron)	5 Staffel (No. 5 Squadron)
3 Staffel (No. 3 Squadron)	6 Staffel (No. 6 Squadron)

With about ten aircraft in each squadron, plus the HQ Staff flights, the total strength of a Bomber Group could be over 100 aircraft. The Heinkel IIIs which operated over the east coast of Scotland were most frequently those of Stab/KG 26, 1/KG 26, 2/KG 26 and 3/KG 26, that is, the HQ Staff flight and Nos 1, 2 and 3 Squadrons of Group 26, the 'Lion' Bomber Group. On either side of the fuselage, near the front of the aircraft, was the profile of a lion on its haunches but alert with its tail raised, and the inscription *Vestigium Leonis* (the tracks of the lion).

On 25 October 1940 a group of Heinkel III bombers attacked the RAF station and the town at Montrose, and the Royal Naval Air station at Arbroath. Attacks were also made on St Andrews and the Cellardyke/Kilrenny areas in Fife. German radio had claimed that the Luftwaffe bombers 'coming from Norway' had successfully attacked two aerodromes in north-east Scotland, Wick and Lossiemouth. The aircraft which attacked Montrose on the evening of 25 October appeared suddenly from over the sea, flying from south-east and south to north-west and north at a very low level (no more than 100 feet). For most eyewitnesses everything was over in a matter of seconds. RAF Montrose was to the north of the town so the bombers attacked the town first as they flew over it on the way to the airfield. There are different accounts of the number of aircraft involved and the type, but the evidence generally supports the view that there were only three aircraft and that they were Heinkel III bombers.

The Tayside police have in their archives reports from the period which give very detailed accounts of the results of the evening's attacks. According to the local police 18 high-explosive bombs were dropped, of which five did not explode. All of the bombs whose weights could accurately be assessed (for example, from unexploded bombs and tail fins found) were reported to be 250 kgs (550 lbs) in weight.

In addition a large number of incendiary bombs were dropped, mostly on the golf links. Several bombs, which were not accounted for by craters, removal or disposal by explosion, were said to have been dropped in the South Esk River between Ferrydean and Montrose. There was also indiscriminate machine gunning of various parts of the town and the airfield. Montrose airfield was badly damaged with a major fire, and six RAF personnel were killed or injured. Two hangars were badly damaged. Seven training aircraft were destroyed and ten damaged, and one light bomber was destroyed

David Birrell was a RAF airframe fitter at Montrose at the time. He recalls that the barrack room was full, with airmen lying on their beds, having finished work for the day. Suddenly they heard the sound of aircraft engines and almost simultaneously the unmistakable chatter of machine gun fire, followed by the crump of bombs exploding. At that moment one of his friends shouted 'Under your beds, fellas!' After a few moments in that position he remembered that he was in charge of stretcher-bearers for that week. The stretchers were located in a small hut between the hangars. What he didn't know was that one of the hangars had received a direct hit which, unfortunately, killed the flight sergeant and two airmen. When he arrived at the hut there was not a soul to be seen and no sign of a stretcher-bearer anywhere. He discovered that the hut was locked with a huge padlock and nobody had issued him with a key. The silence was now deafening and everyone seemed to be waiting for a rerun which, fortunately, did not take place. Minutes later there was pandemonium as everyone got stuck into clearing up the debris.

12 The battles of the raiders

In many ways, the surface raiders shared the problems and some of the methods of the early pirates of the classic age of piracy in the 17th and early 18th centuries. They used disguises to approach their prey – the pirates used false flags in a very similar fashion. They constantly used their captured prizes to survive and move on to the next kill. Again, this echoes the practices of the pirates of old, who always sought supplies as much as treasure and loot. They opened fire on their enemies at the last possible moment, and used intimidation to force a quick surrender, again, following the methods of their predecessors. Bernhard Rogge's clandestine repairs at the Kerguelen Islands echoed the many pirates who careened and refitted their ships in secluded inlets.

What perhaps separates the raiders of the two eras is that the German raiders were ready to fight. The old-fashioned pirates avoided a fight whenever possible – their real objective was always money. (One of the few exceptions is the final battle of Blackbeard against the British frigate *Scarborough*, which resulted in his defeat and death.) But the German raiders often fought hard, and often against superior force, although they were under order to avoid fight!

Before passing on to the tales of those German ships, there is an interesting anecdote of a remarkable incident involving two Allied ships and two Japanese raiders:

Japanese raiders put in their appearance in 1942, and were only three in number, two of which were the *Aikoku Maru* and the *Hokoku Maru*. The *Hokoku Maru* and another Japanese raider were cruising in the Indian Ocean in November 1942 and encountered the Dutch tanker *Ondina* and her escort, the Indian minesweeper *Bengal*. The latter vessel carried one 12-pounder gun and the *Ondina* one 4-inch, manned by a single Australian seaman. The two Japanese ships carried six 5.5-inch guns each, and therefore disposed of a broadside of 640 lb against the 43 lb 'throw-weight' of their two opponents.

The *Bengal* saw the two raiders early in the morning, at about 5.30 a.m. and immediately made for the larger ship, hoping to cover the tanker's escape. The *Ondina* did not take this opportunity, but also attacked the enemy with her one gun, mounted on her stern. The *Hokoku Maru* caught fire after the *Bengal* had hit her twice, then she exploded and sank an hour after the action had been joined. The *Bengal* immediately steamed off to help the *Ondina*. She fired with her one gun until she had used up all but five rounds of ammunition. After that, she retreated and put up smoke, trying to induce the other Japanese raider to follow. However, the raider was not to be drawn, and she fought the *Ondina* until the latter ran out of ammunition, whereupon her crew abandoned ship and were machine gunned in the water by the raider's crew. Nobody was hit but one of the survivors said that the Japanese must have just been entertaining themselves; otherwise all the targets would have been dead.

The *Aikoku Maru* fired two torpedoes at the tanker, went off to pick up the survivors of the *Hokoku Maru*, after which she fired another torpedo at the tanker which was listing to one side, and having missed again, *Aikoku Maru* departed. The survivors then went back to the *Ondina*, put her in order, put out a fire, and brought their ship into Fremantle seven days later. The whole encounter was later described as miraculous. One smaller ship, armed with one 12-pounder gun, had engaged two raiders, both larger vessels, sunk one of them and enabled their charge, the tanker, to escape, and had then escaped herself: an extraordinary outcome.

Bernhard Rogge's defiance of a British heavy cruiser has already been discussed. However, there were a number of other instances. One involved Ship 10, the *Thor*, which was one of the smaller vessels working as an auxiliary cruiser.

Thor: Ship 10

The *Thor* had begun life as the banana boat *Santa Cruz*, and was built by the shipbuilders Deutsche Werft of Hamburg for the Oldenburg-Portuguesische Line in 1938.

It is interesting to note that the German High Naval Command, the Seekriegsleitung, or SKL, were always interested in vessels designed for carrying fruit, because they made excellent merchant raiders. Fruit-carrying boats were fast (to minimize deterioration in their fragile cargo) and small – and thus presented a smaller target to an adversary. There is even a possibility, though not a proven one, that under the Weimar Republic, financial assistance was given to banana plantations deliberately in order that these firms could order ships which could be made into raiders in the event of war.

The *Thor* had oil-fired steam turbines in her engine-room, which could propel her at a maximum of 17 knots, and could travel 40,000 miles at a speed of 10 knots before refuelling. She was captained by Otto Kahler, who was 49 years old, and a professional navy man. He had commanded both of the German navy's training ships which were sailing vessels.

The *Thor* left Kiel on 6 June 1940. She was escorted out into the Atlantic with a heavy escort, to make sure that she got a good start. She was masquerading as a Russian ship, the *Orsk*. She was fortunate in that the weather was very bad which aided her concealment. She was out into the open Atlantic by 16 June, and passed over several early possible victims, in one case because the captain suspected that the ship in question was an armed merchant cruiser, and in others because Kahler did not wish to draw attention to himself too soon.

After that, the *Thor* began her work. She captured the Dutch vessel, the *Kertosono*, with a single warning shot, and sent her back to Lorient with a prize crew. After that the *Delambre*, a British ship under charter to the Admiralty, was taken and scuttled. She had carried cotton, hides and cotton seed.

On 9 July, Kahler took and scuttled the *Bruges*, a Belgian ship, and scuttled that also. Five days later he took the *Gracefield*, which was also sunk.

This smooth run of luck was somewhat marred two days later, when they stopped the *Wendover*, a coal-carrying ship taking her cargo to Buenos Aires. They sent off a radio alarm and tried to man the guns. Their attempt at resistance failed, and they were sunk. It is worth mentioning that in spite of their attempt at defiance, the crew were taken prisoner, and the two fatalities were buried at sea with military honours, their bodies covered by the British flag. The following day, they captured and sank the *Tela*. They had 194 prisoners on board, and were growing rather crowded.

On 28 July, a big ship was sighted. It was either a large cargo ship or an armed merchant cruiser. She was moving at 16 knots, which suggested she was, in fact, a cargo-carrier. Kahler moved in on her. At one minute past ten in the morning the siren sounded, and the *Thor* sent her crew to action stations and changed course, moving at 17 knots. The other ship changed course to meet her. It could now be seen that she was about 14,000 tons burden, with elevated upperworks, and it was obvious to Kahler that she was an armed merchant cruiser. Kahler had specific orders to try to avoid any shooting match with enemy warships. His job was to raid commerce and to disrupt and sink shipping. Accordingly, he fled at full speed, with the British ship about 20,000 yards in his rear.

The chase went on for several hours, until past noon. At last the pursuing ship, the *Alcantara*, which was in fact larger than estimated at 20,000 tons, and was speedy, being a former Royal Mail liner, began to gain on the *Thor*. She also sent out a lengthy message in code, which could not be read. Kahler realized he had to either fight or surrender. He decided to fight, and dropped her disguise at 12.57 p.m. He also reduced speed to 15 knots, since the higher speed at which he had been running caused intense vibration in the ship, and made range-finding and sighting difficult. He ran round at right angles across bows of the *Alcantara*, hoisted the German flag and opened fire with a four-gun broadside at a range of 14,000 yards.

The *Alcantara*, whose crew had probably gone to action stations as soon as the *Thor* had been sighted, fired back immediately, and turned, so that she could use her starboard broadside. The German ship had the advantage in that the sun was shining over them direct into the eyes of the British gunners. The *Alcantara* was hit twice – once between the bridge and the funnel, and once aft. The next round of fire from the *Thor* cut the fire-control wire of the No. 4 gun and killed one man, and the next hit the *Alcantara* below the water-line. This was not too serious, but water entered the hull and the drag reduced her speed.

The firing went on, and Kahler altered course and increased his speed. He wanted to break off the action as soon as possible. However, he found that he could not reach full speed (this was due to technical troubles with his condenser) and the *Thor* was hit for the first time. The shell went right through the ship without exploding. However, it tore away electric cables which powered the ammunition hoists for the forward guns. This damage was repaired fairly quickly, but soon after a shell burst on the starboard side on the boat-deck. There were splinters flung hither and thither. The starboard torpedo tubes were put out of action.

The *Thor* was steering south, and seemed to be going faster than her enemy – probably because of the lucky shot which had let water into the *Alcantara*'s hull. Kahler took care to turn dead astern relative to the British vessel, so that his ship presented a smaller target. He also continued to return the enemy's fire, though his own smoke and the fact that his fire-control position was masked by his own funnel hindered this to quite a large extent. The *Alcantara* was still firing, but shortly after one o'clock Kahler had to cease replying. He realized that the target was now completely hidden by the smoke, and he was merely wasting his shells. He manoeuvred his ship out of the smoke and opened fire once more, but no hits could be seen. When the smoke cleared, the *Alcantara* was firing, but stationary.

A few minutes later Kahler stopped the action and steamed away. He said later he would have liked to go back and finish his enemy, but he had used a lot of his ammunition (2,084 5.9-inch shells) and his orders were specific – namely, to avoid action. (This decision was later approved by Admiral Raeder.) He was left to bury his dead and change his disguise, which was now useless.

This was not the last serious action which his ship had to meet. In December of the same year, Kahler was cruising south of the River Plate. On 5 December 1940, a ship emerged out of a bank of fog, about four miles away. She was a very big ship, and was in fact the *Carnarvon Castle*, an armed merchant cruiser. It signalled to the *Thor*, asking the German ship to identify itself, but Kahler ignored it, and steamed on, hoping to lose the British ship in the fog.

It was just past 7 a.m. when the *Carnarvon Castle* opened fire, and Kahler immediately replied. The British ship lay to southward and Kahler began to emulate the manoeuvre which had worked well in the case of the *Alcantara*, namely to work his ship around so that the sun shone into the British gunners' eyes.

The British ship kept up its fire, using four 6 inch guns, one forward by the bow, another just forward of the mainmast, and one at the stern. They also used two smaller guns behind the funnel on the boat deck. The *Carnarvon Castle* chased the *Thor* northwards, and after a few minutes the two ships were circling, each around the other. *Thor* fired two torpedoes, which both missed. However, the range was now much shorter, and Kahler's guns kept on firing as the distance between the two ships went down to 7,000 yards. The British ship was hit by these constant salvoes, and sustained five hits; but managed to maintain her speed, and fired, albeit irregularly, managing to turn east and keep all her broadside at work.

This intense action went on for an hour, until Kahler had to consider a novel problem. He was worried that ammunition was running low; to add to which, several of his guns were so hot from constant firing that their mountings had jammed, hindering aiming. He was considering this when the British ship, to his great surprise, broke of the action, and made off north, without hitting the *Thor* even once. In fact, though Kahler did not know this, the *Carnarvon Castle* was in a very bad way. She was on fire, the anti-aircraft magazine was flooded, and only 40 rounds of ammunition was unused. In addition, there was a cordite fire at number four 6 inch gun, as well as a fire around the funnel. Nor was that all: the main engine's exhaust was useless and 40 per cent of her exposed personnel were casualties, and she had two hits in the hull just above the water line. So the *Carnarvon Castle* steamed away, listing to port, to obtain emergency repairs in Montevideo. Ironically, her hull was patched with plates from the *Graf Spee*, which had scuttled there in 1939.

Kahler was not exactly free of trouble. He had used up 70 per cent of his ammunition but he was undamaged. He received a congratulatory message from the SKL, the high command, but they both knew that he had been very lucky indeed. However, supply ships soon arrived, and Kahler and his ship's crew had a triumphant Christmas.

The *Thor* set off to cruise in the South Atlantic, and on 22 March sank the passenger liner *Britannia*. There is no doubt that this sinking (Kahler did not pick up the crew and passengers from her boats, since there was a British warship approaching) was a black mark on Kahler's record, of which he was aware, since he tried to excuse himself on various grounds – that he did not know she was a passenger ship, and (contradictorily) that she was a troop transport.

After that the *Thor* went on its way until, at 6.15 a.m. on 4 April, heavy smoke was sighted on the south-west horizon. Masts and a funnel could also be seen and Kahler went to check her out, putting up a Greek flag as he did so. At 6.45 he hoisted the German flag and put a shot across the bows of the oncoming ship, only to see at the same moment two guns on her prow, mounted on the forecastle. It was another armed British merchant cruiser, and a moment later Kahler opened fire with every gun that could be brought to bear. They hit with the first salvo, and within three minutes the British ship, the *Voltaire*, was seriously afire, at first admidships, although at times it seemed to encompass the entire ship.

At that point the *Thor* lost her radio aerial, the only damage she sustained in the entire action. Single guns were firing from the *Voltaire*. Kahler turned his ship away, thinking that his adversary might try to torpedo him. The *Voltaire* began to circle and soon it was apparent that her steering gear was jammed, and she was now on fire from end to end. However, gun flashes from prow and stern showed that they were still firing.

The *Thor* sent out a torpedo, and then turned to engage his enemy with the other guns in broadside firing mode. Three guns hit the *Voltaire* again and again until they broke down, after which the only possibility was to manoeuvre the ship and try to use a torpedo once again. However, at this point, the *Voltaire* ceased firing and ran up a white flag. The *Thor* approached the beaten vessel as closely as she could without running into danger, and picked up as many of the crew that were already in the water.

At about half-past eight the *Voltaire* sank, with a huge cloud of smoke going up and leaving a large oil-patch behind. The action was over. It had lasted slightly under an hour and the *Thor* had fired 724 rounds – more than half its ammunition supply. It stayed at the scene of the action, picking up all the survivors possible. There were 197 of these, including the captain and 19 officers.

After this the *Thor* completed her cruise and came home safely.

Kormoran: Ship 41

The last that was heard of the *Kormoran* was when she was refuelled and her stores replenished. Her sphere of action was the Indian Ocean, and her captain was Captain Theodor Detmers, who had taken up his command at the age of 38, which made him the youngest of the raider captains.

The stores had been brought to him by the *Kulmerland* (namely 4,000 tons of diesel fuel, lubricating oil, white metal and provisions for six months). She also took off the prisoners which the *Kormoran* had taken. The *Kulmerland* left Kobe on 3 September 1940, and left the *Kormoran* fully supplied up until 1 June 1942.

For information about what happened next the German naval command had to rely on letters received later from Detmers when he became a prisoner of the Allies in Australia. Apparently Detmers, who had been going to lay mines off Perth, changed his mind when he heard that there were plans for a big convoy to leave that city, escorted by the British cruiser *Cornwall*.

His plans were interrupted when, on 19 November 1940, smoke was sighted ahead of the *Kormoran*'s bow. Soon a light cruiser, which in fact was the *Sydney*, was seen heading directly towards them. The *Kormoran* immediately turned away and began a run for it, travelling at 18 knots. The *Sydney* was faster, moving at perhaps 25 knots. Detmers hoisted the Dutch flag, and answered the *Sydney* searchlight signals by means of flags. (This was quite usual practice in the merchant service generally.) Detmers gained time by answering the signals deliberately sloppily. Some of them were incorrect, and he sometimes replied to the *Sydney* by simply sending the message 'Not understood'.

Soon the *Sydney* was very near the *Kormoran*. By all the usual rules, there should have been no doubt about what happened next. The *Sydney* was by far the more powerful ship and many captains would have hesitated before engaging her in combat. However, Detmers had long considered what he should do if a more powerful vessel tried to engage him, and he now put his plans into action.

It was 5.30 p.m. when the *Sydney* came up, side by side with the *Kormoran*, and was about 900 yards away from the *Kormoran*'s starboard side. The seaplane the *Sydney* carried had been slung out over the side, but it did not seem that she was expecting action. Apart from anything else, only about half the gun-crews seemed to be at action stations. It was at this point that the *Sydney* demanded the *Kormoran*'s secret call sign – that is, her identification as a Dutch vessel, which she had adopted as a disguise. Of course, this could not be given, and Detmers decided to fight. The guns cleared for action in six seconds, and up went the German flag, which was hardly in place when the *Kormoran* opened fire. The second salvo, fired from three guns, scored hits on the fire-control command post and the bridge of the Australian ship.

The *Sydney* now opened fire, but the shells went soaring over the *Kormoran* to fall harmlessly in the sea. In the meantime, the *Kormoran* scored more hits on both forward gun-turrets, blowing the top off the other. Immediately afterwards, the *Kormoran* destroyed the seaplane which the *Sydney* had swung out, ready for use. (The German ship was firing at very close range, and could hardly miss.) After this, there were more disasters for the *Sydney*. A torpedo from the *Kormoran* hit her forward, and the resultant inrush of water began to pull down her bow, causing her to lose speed. The *Kormoran* used her 37-millimetre anti-tank gun and her 20-millimetre anti-aircraft guns to dominate the decks of the *Sydney*. No fire-control ratings or the men who were to man the torpedo tubes could get to their stations, and they took heavy casualties.

It was only now that the two guns the *Sydney* had left to use actually began to hit back. They were the guns of the two turrets at her stern. They hit the *Kormoran* at three points. The first was the wireless room, where two men were killed and the second was a hit on the auxiliary boiler room and the oil bunker. This made the ship's fire-fighting equipment useless. The transformers attached to the main engines were also damaged, and two crew members at the No 3 gun were injured. A heavy fire started in the engine-room, and the electrical gear began to fail. The engine-room staff endeavoured to put out the fire, but were all killed.

The *Sydney* dropped astern, crippled by her injuries, but the captain, still full of fighting spirit, tried to ram the *Kormoran*, which was now obviously out of the control of her crew. *Sydney* fired off four torpedoes, all of which missed. The *Sydney* was now steaming very slowly, at only 5 or 6 knots, and her guns were jammed in a position which pointed away from her opponent. The German shells were hitting her continuously around the water line, every four or five seconds. (In all, the *Kormoran* fired about 500 rounds in this engagement.)

This fierce engagement only lasted half an hour, when the *Sydney* decided that she had had enough. She was heavily ablaze, and there were constant explosions in her hull, probably from her own stored ammunition. She was now 10,000 yards from the *Kormoran*, and out of range. She steamed away, still on fire, and the German crew watched her go. The fire from her hull was visible until 11 p.m., and it was then that she probably sank.

However, the *Kormoran* was hardly in better condition, and Detmers was forced to order the crew to abandon ship, though for some time the gun-crews stayed at their posts. Rafts and rubber dinghies had to be pressed into service since some of the boats had been destroyed by enemy fire. Two steel lifeboats survived, but were in the No. 1 hold, from which they were hauled up by hand.

About 20 men had been killed during the fight. As the ship's crew left the sinking *Kormoran*, a big rubber dinghy sank, drowning some 60 more. The fire crept nearer to the stored mines. At 1 a.m. Detmers hauled down the flag and his captain's pennant and abandoned ship. The *Kormoran* sank some 20 minutes later, after the stored mines at last exploded.

Now in the boats, the men had to endure worsening weather conditions as the various rafts and dinghies drifted apart. In the end, they were lucky. A coasting steamer picked up one boatload, and the resultant alarm gave rise to a search which brought all the surviving Germans to safety, though they all suffered greatly from heat and cold. One raft was so crowded that the occupants had to take turns in sitting and standing. There were 57 men on it, and nobody could lie down.

There were no survivors from the *Sydney*. Naval opinion afterwards held that the captain of the Australian ship was at fault for approaching a suspicious ship far too closely. He had also come towards her on a bearing which gave a favourable field of fire for her guns and torpedoes, a recipe for disaster.

Stier: Ship 26

Perhaps the most outstanding action by a raider should be given pride of place at the end of this chapter. It was the action between the *Stier* (Ship 26) and the *Stephen Hopkins*. At the time the *Stier* was cruising the River Plate–Cape Town shipping lane.

> Gerlach, the captain of the *Stier*, had just made a rendezvous with the *Michel* (Ship 28) and the *Tannenfels*, a German blockade runner. The *Michel* had made off, and the *Stier* and the *Tannenfels* were keeping company for a few days, while the former cleaned the ship's sides and did some urgent painting work. It was the morning of 27th September 1941. The wind began to get up, and the ship's executive officer brought the men engaged in painting back on board, not wishing for any of his crew to be overboard in case an enemy ship approached them unobserved, although, in fact, they were in an area where very few ships came. There appears to have been no hurry about this order, however, and the men just came on board when they had finished the jobs they had in hand. By 8.50 am only a few men were still on stagings over the side and still working. Visibility was narrowing, however, and was about two to two and a quarter miles.
>
> It was then that a ship, soon perceived to be a large vessel, came into sight, hoisting a signal which read, 'Stop at once.' Captain Gerlach immediately ordered full speed ahead. Two minutes after that the anti-aircraft guns asked permission to open fire and a minute later the main guns were also ready to open fire.
>
> The *Stier* actually began firing at 8.56 am, and four minutes later the unidentified enemy (who was actually the *Stephen Hopkins*, an American Liberty ship, armed with a single 4-inch gun). What followed has been described as 'one of the great single-ship actions of all time.'

The *Stephen Hopkins* turned to port, the *Stier* to starboard, to stop the American escaping. As the *Stier* did so, she was hit twice by the shells from the American. The resulting damage was severe, and as a result her helm was jammed in the 'hardastarboard' position. Simultaneously, the supply of oil was cut to the engine-room. Since the *Stier* was turning at the time, she came round (with the momentum of her movement) far enough for her to use her port broadside. Gerlach also tried to use torpedoes, but failed, simply because the electrical supply throughout the ship was out of action. Even the guns had difficulty. The power hoists which brought up the ammunition were not working, so shells and charges had to be brought up by human labour.

In spite of all these problems, the *Stier* continued firing at a very respectable rate, and soon started several fires on board the *Stephen Hopkins*. Just after 9 a.m., a rain squall came down and obscured visibility to such an extent that the *Stier* ceased firing for a while, but when visibility improved the firing continued, with the result that by 9.20 a.m. both ships were lying near each other, crippled and motionless. The *Stephen Hopkins* was the worse injured, and sank at 10 a.m.

Gerlach now had to consider his position. His ship was severely damaged – burning oil was drifting about the engine-room, and the fire had spread out of the engine-room to burn anything, such as bunks, bedding and furniture. The hand fire-extinguishers were used, since the heavier fire-fighting equipment was out of action, and the fire spread unchecked throughout the ship. It was not really surprising, since the *Stier* had been hit 15 times.

The hand-extinguishers soon emptied, and were supplemented by tubs, buckets and even whole lifeboats full of water that were lowered over the side, sunk and hoisted inboard again by the crew. This could not stop the fire spreading and the flames began to get near the No 2 hold, where 19 torpedoes were stored.

The only remedy was to flood this hold. Unfortunately the flooding valves could not be reached, and the torpedo crews (who supervised the torpedoes release in action) were trapped below in the 'tween decks, their escape barred by more flames.

The torpedo officer managed to rescue his men, which was a very brave act and by 10.14 a.m. the engines were working again. However, the rudder was still jammed and the engines worked only for ten minutes before they broke down again. There was a conference of all the officers on the bridge. As it took place, the men manning the auxiliary steering gear were driven away by the heat.

The decision was a fairly obvious one. The ship was unmanageable, and the decks were becoming red-hot. The crew began to abandon ship, lowering their boats and rafts into the water while the *Tannenfels* stood by. She picked up the men from the water and the *Stier* blew up a few minutes later. The survivors, by now standing on the deck of the *Tannenfels*, watched her go down.

The crew had lost three men and 33 were wounded. The survivors on board the *Tannenfels* reached Bordeaux on 8 November.

As for the *Stephen Hopkins*, only 15 survived. They reached Brazil after a journey in one of the ship's boats, taking 31 days. The rest (41 men) died in the wreck of their ship. They had put up a terrific fight, almost certainly unique in the history of the Second World War and perhaps in the whole history of naval warfare. The German vessel had an overwhelming superiority in terms of guns – firing a 400 lb broadside as against a 31 lb broadside from the American ship. The *Stier* had a fully trained naval crew, while the *Stephen Hopkins* was a merchant ship having only a squad of naval reservists manning her gun. Lastly, the *Stier* had a modern fire-control system, which the *Stephen Hopkins* completely lacked. There is no doubt that the crew showed exceptional bravery and determination.

13 Three raider commanders

It would now be useful to glance at the personalities and conduct of three very different raider commanders. While it is true to say that raider warfare was, by its nature, a more ruthless business than ordinary combat, there were, nevertheless, degrees in this lack of mercy and human feeling. This is illustrated by the following biographical sketches:

Captain Bernard Rogge

Rogge commanded the *Atlantis*, whose former name was the *Goldenfels*, which was referred to as 'Schip 16' by German Intelligence. Rogge seems to have been, from the start, an outstanding commander. His men respected him and responded well to his command. He demanded strict discipline in their operations, and the men respected this regime.

It is interesting to note the way that he operated. When he approached his prey, he would open fire firstly with the 75-millimetre gun (which was mounted aft), or sometimes with a single 5.9-inch – then with a half-broadside of 5.9-inch guns and (if necessary) following that up with all the guns at his disposal. Later on, when Allied ships sailing alone grew very suspicious and super-vigilant, Rogge realized that this somewhat leisurely routine was too lengthy. The main problem was that he could not afford to chase a victim, since that would give the ship concerned time to send out a warning. He adopted a more ruthless routine, but he laid down that the firing should only continue until the enemy wireless was destroyed – after which the prey were to be given a chance to survive by surrendering.

Although Rogge was ruthless to his victims if they disobeyed his orders, the crucial one being that when approached they made no signal which would invite a rescue, he tried to be humane in other ways. If he took prisoners on board his ship he did his best for them before transferring them to a prison ship. There was one tragedy involving prisoners which he had taken, but it does not seem to have been Rogge's fault. He had captured the Yugoslav vessel *Tirrana*, which he used as a prison ship, and 87 captives were sent aboard her to a neutral port. On the way, the *Tirrana* was sunk by HMS *Tuna*, probably through a misunderstanding between port officials and the German crew of the *Tirrana*. The prisoners were locked below, and drowned.

Rogge cruised successfully until December 1940, when the *Atlantis* arrived at the Kerguelen Islands. These islands are bleak, treeless, and very cold, being not far from the Antarctic. It is possible that Rogge went there with the specific purpose of giving his crew a Christmas rest. However, as they were arriving at the island a serious accident occurred. The *Atlantis* was entering Gazelle Bay but as she was doing so, she can aground on the rocks. The first attempts to get her out of her predicament failed. Divers were sent down, and they came up to say that there were holes in the hull in the area of the forepeak and also in the forward compartments of the double bottom. It took 30 hours of hard work before the ship could be freed. She was listed from side to side by shifting weight, and her engines were run full speed, both ahead and astern. In the end she was kedged off – but it was a serious problem which had to be addressed immediately.

Firstly, however, they had to check their situation. The ship's plane was launched, and it surveyed the island. Fortunately for Rogge, it was completely uninhabited. A regular watch had to be maintained to seaward, in case other ships approached. In addition, a gunnery observation post and fire control was set up ashore which ensured that the ship's guns could fire over the mountains at any enemy who approached, without themselves being seen. That done, the main body of the work was commenced. The damage suffered when entering Gazelle Bay was repaired which took a fortnight of uninterrupted diving as the collision with the rocks had resulted in extensive damage. Some of the central plating of the keel had been torn off, and a large area of the ship's bottom was dented. The ship possessed an underwater oxyacetylene cutter, but this was out of order. As a result, the damaged plates had to be dealt with individually. They were drilled and then pulled out by the ship's capstan. The missing part of the keel was repaired by substituting a paravane spar. Rogge, who was always a thorough and conscientious captain, put on a diving suit and checked the progress of the whole process.

The crew also carried out a general overhaul of the ship. Not only that, but the disguise was changed, and the whole ship repainted. Rogge took the opportunity to allow his crew some recreation. They were all allowed ashore, which they must have welcomed. By this time they had been at sea since the preceding March – nine months ago. They took full advantage of the opportunity. They hunted rabbits and duck, and collected sea-shells and Kerguelen cabbage. There was fresh water, and a pipeline half a mile long was rigged to run drinking water to the ship. At Christmas, there was a very big party, and every member of the crew got a present, which was taken from some of the booty seized from the *Automedon*, one of the ships which had fallen prey to her.

Repairs completed, the *Atlantis* left Gazelle Bay, after a stay of 26 days but it was not all plain sailing. In May they had a very narrow escape indeed from complete disaster. Around the 17th of the month the *Atlantis* was drifting. (The ability to do this was an immense advantage – if the *Atlantis* had been steam-powered, the engines would have had to be kept turning all the time, to ensure readiness if action was called for.)

While the *Atlantis* was lying like this, motionless and completely silent, the outlines of two large ships were seen through the night. They were coming directly towards her so she slowly started her engines, to avoid sparks from the funnel which would have drawn the attention of the unknown vessels. The log of the *Atlantis* records that the night was not completely dark. By the light of the moon the crew of the *Atlantis* saw that they were facing two large warships. The log identifies them as a battleship of the Nelson Class and an Eagle Class aircraft-carrier.

It must have been a very daunting moment with escape seeming quite impossible. Fortunately, however, for Rogge and his men the moon was behind the British ships. The *Atlantis*, from their point of view, was difficult to see, since it stood against a dark, hazy background. Rogge took the decision to move away, slowly increasing speed, while the British ships passed by about 7,000 yards away. It worked – the British ships disappeared over the horizon and the *Atlantis* was alone again.

A few days later, on 21 May, Rogge attacked a Greek ship at night. However, she at once surrendered and convinced Rogge that she was under charter to Switzerland, and was accordingly released, but was warned not to use her wireless.

Three days after that, the *Atlantis* nearly met disaster when she attacked a ship at night. It was the 4,350-ton *Trafalgar*, carrying 4,500 tons of coal and two aircraft. The 5.9-inch guns opened on her. The searchlights illuminated the prey with the first salvo setting the ship on fire, followed by another five. The aircraft, which were carried in crates as deck cargo, burst into flames. The funnel and mast collapsed, and the crew took to their boats. However, the *Trafalgar* was not finished yet. With her helm jammed, she steamed round in circles, and there was a possibility that she might ram the *Atlantis*, which fired a torpedo to sink the burning ship at once. However, the torpedo's gyro failed and it turned and made back towards the *Atlantis*, which now found herself menaced by the burning ship and the torpedo simultaneously. In fact, the torpedo narrowly missed, and two more torpedoes had to be fired before the *Trafalgar* sank. The survivors of the attack were picked up by Rogge's men who found, no doubt to their relief, that the British had not had time to give the alarm.

After several more successful actions in the Atlantic, the German high command decided that it was time for the *Atlantis* to move on. There were several reasons for this decision – the main one being that she had now notched up 21 successful actions. A good deal of information had reached the British about the ship, and the situation was further complicated by the loss of the German battleship *Bismarck* and the capture of nine of the supply ships which had been servicing the raider fleet.

As a result of all this, the *Atlantis* was ordered to the Pacific, round the Cape of Good Hope, where they ran through a hurricane and the *Atlantis* had to heave to. After that she sailed on for four weeks in remote seas, far from the usual shipping routes. The crew had been expecting to head for home before this, and had reacted extremely well, but Rogge was careful to keep them very busy, overhauling all the equipment on board.

In the end, she reached her rendezvous with her supply ship, the *Münsterland*. She was accompanied by the *Silvaplana*, a prize which she had taken on the way. There she met Ship No. 45, the *Komet*, which was commanded by Rear Admiral Robert Eyssen. There was a disagreement between himself and Rogge over the division of the available supplies. In spite of the fact that Rogge was junior in rank, he seems to have held his own in the matter. In the end, the *Atlantis* headed off north-east, aiming in the direction of the Pomotu Archipelago and (afterwards) Pitcairn Island. They made landfall at Vanavana, in the Pomotu group, and the crew were able to have shore leave again and go surf bathing.

On 18 October Rogge decided that they should start off on the voyage home. To do this they would go round Cape Horn and they plan was that the were to rendezvous with a U-boat, *U-68*. They were to meet her at a point 500 miles south of St Helena. They were to refuel her, and then go to refuel the *U-126* off Ascension Island.

On 8 November the crew celebrated completing the voyage around the world, and on the 13th they met the *U-68*. Rogge took advantage of this break in the journey to change the disguise of the ship. The crew made a thorough job, using the flooding tanks on one side and then the other to paint their ship down to the water line. Then she moved on to her meeting with the *U-126* which was made on 22 November. The commander came on board the *Atlantis* with some of his crew, and enjoyed, having the luxury of hot baths, unobtainable on board a submarine.

The two boats were drifting together, carrying out their business, when there was an alarm. A heavy British cruiser was in sight. The *U-126* lost no time. She cut her line and the refuelling hose and dived very hurriedly, so hurriedly, in fact, that the captain and the crew were left behind on board the *Atlantis*. Even in this emergency, she did her best to protect the submarine, swinging the hull so that it would screen the submarine from the view of the cruiser and any plane it might launch.

Rogge was in a fix. The enemy ship was of the London Class, and had eight 8-inch guns. Not only was she by far the more powerful ship, but she was 14 knots faster than the German vessel, so they could not run away from her. All they could do was to try to lure her within reach of their guns and torpedoes.

The cruiser was the *Devonshire*, skippered by Captain R. D. Oliver. As soon as she was in range, she immediately opened fire but at first the shells fell short. *Atlantis*, very cheekily, tried to trick the *Devonshire* by transmitting the signal 'RRR'. This meant 'I am being attacked by a surface vessel' and of course they hoped that the *Devonshire* would think she had attacked a friendly vessel, and would go on her way with apologies. The *Atlantis* further identified herself as the British ship *Polyphemus*. The British naval authorities were ahead of them, however. Knowing that the raider ships would probably know the British signals, they had recently changed them. The signal should have been four letters, 'RRRR' and not just three.

In addition, the plane which the British cruiser launched spotted the vast oil patch left behind by the *U-126*. The *Atlantis* was challenged by radio, and replied innocently 'What do you want?' In the meantime, the British cruiser stayed well out of range, about 17,000 yards away. Then the seaplane reported that the ship they were looking at had the wrong-shaped stern to be the genuine *Polyphemus* – curved instead of straight. That settled it. The *Devonshire* opened fire and sent three 8-inch salvoes against the *Atlantis*. The first missed entirely, but one shell from the second held the prow, and then the third set the *Atlantis*'s plane on fire. Rogge ordered smoke to be made, and under that cover the boats and rafts were lowered, and the crew abandoned ship leaving two men who had been killed. Shortly after Rogge left, the last man to do so, the magazine exploded and his ship sank in two minutes.

Rogge and his men began to prepare for a long period in the lifeboats. With characteristic energy, the captain told the men to collect pieces of wreckage. These were lashed together and formed rafts for the men who had no place in the boats. It was found that there were actually seven missing, including the two killed in the assault.

While this was going on, they had a pleasant surprise when U-boat surfaced again. Her lieutenant had taken charge in the captain's absence and the stranded crew had some help. The problem was that there were too many of them to be taken aboard the submarine, which was very short of accommodation. In the end, some were taken on board, while another group in life jackets, sat on deck. If the submarine had to dive, they would have to be ready to swim. Another group sat in the boats and on the rafts, which were towed. The submarine headed for Pernambuco.

It was a very difficult journey. The lines to the boats and rafts broke continuously until eventually there was no spare rope left. The three groups swapped places regularly, but it was very difficult, for many of the men were wearing only shorts, and suffered badly from the cold. However, it was over in 38 hours, although it must have seemed much longer to those involved. In spite of all the difficulties, everyone had the chance for a hot meal – the chef of the submarine seemed to have worked overtime.

Admiral Doenitz himself organized the subsequent rescue which was a complicated business. The supply ship *Python* was teamed up with three submarines and ordered to rescue the men of the *Atlantis*, which was done on the night of 23/24 November. After that, the *Python* went on with the business of supplying the U-boats. On 1 December the supply ship and its attendant submarines were on the surface when the *Dorsetshire*, a three-funnelled cruiser and sister ship of the *Devonshire*, appeared. The submarines all crash-dived. The *U-68* had some difficulty – she had open hatches since she had been loading torpedoes at the time. Another submarine, the *U-A*, attacked the *Dorsetshire* but her torpedoes missed, and the *Python* had to scuttle herself.

History then repeated itself. After the *Dorsetshire* had gone, the submarines surfaced and began to pick up the pieces. There was the crew of the *Python* and most of the men from the *Atlantis*. They found there were 414 men to look after. Each submarine took 100 men, and the rest were towed in ten lifeboats. Doenitz then had to organize another rescue operation. He sent eight submarines, four of which were Italian. They went down into the Atlantic and brought everyone back to safety. On the way, the *U-124* sank the British cruiser *Dunedin*.

On New Year's Day 1942 the survivors of the *Atlantis* were entertained in Berlin by Hitler, and Rogge received the Oak Leaves to his Knight's Cross. He had accomplished great things: he had sunk or made prize 22 ships, a total of 145,697 tons; he had sailed round the world, a voyage of 102,000 miles and been at sea for 622 days. After this he did not return to active service but was given a desk job. In the course of this, he laid down some of the principles which had enabled him to do so well. One basic rule he made was that only men who had a skilled trade in civilian life should serve aboard the raiders. Unskilled men, he said, were too easily demoralized.

He said that the choice of ship's doctors was very important. The two medical men he had on board the *Atlantis* had functioned very well as unofficial counsellors – the crew trusted them and confided in them more than they felt able to do with the executive officers. Rogge was very aware of the necessity to keep up morale and allow an outlet for grievances.

His crew's mental state was a constant concern, and he employed many means to uphold it. Any good news for members of the crew, such as a promotion, was always publicly posted on a special 'good news' board. There was a ship's newspaper, using the radio reports of the German official news agency. There were many amateur theatrical presentations and model-making, always a sailor's hobby, was encouraged. There were many other diversions. Courses in mathematics, English, history, political economy and typewriting were available. Sunday was always observed (subject to naval emergency) as a day of rest. The ship carried a store of quality gramophone records. There was a band, though Rogge admitted its quality was not high, but there were frequent singsongs, especially when tropical weather permitted them to be held on deck. Another important practice was that the food was always exactly the same for officers and men, and any luxuries, whether obtained from prizes or otherwise, were also equally shared by all ranks.

In addition, Rogge devised a unique system of 'leave on board'. The crew (in groups of 12) took eight days off. They made use of the isolation hospital, where they could divert themselves as they pleased, writing either poetry or fiction, playing games, reading, sunbathing, whatever they liked. During this time they stepped out of the ship's life except during meals – or, of course, during emergencies. In this case, officers and petty officers were granted an additional favour – they could take their leave in their cabins. (This was probably allowed because crew members would have felt inhibited if they were socializing with their superiors.) This arrangement was not uncommon – nearly everyone had two leaves like this during the voyage.

Rogge recommended, in addition, that a raider should appear in a certain area, wreak havoc, and then move on. By so doing, he would force the enemy to move in convoy constantly, which wasted so much time and effort that it was as good as continued sinkings. The raider thus survived, and was effective merely by being a threat. He also recommended that when the ship was finally unable to operate, the ship's crew should go ashore and make war on land, attacking the enemy's colonies, which had been done in the First World War by the captain of the *Königsberg*.

Rogge took up his appointment as Director of Officers' Training and Education at Kiel in April 1942. He ended the war as Doenitz's immediate aide, as a vice-admiral.

It is pleasant to be able to say that Rogge was not the only captain who endeavoured to carry out his unpleasant duties as humanely as possible. Naval historian Captain S.W. Roskill, DSC, RN, wrote in *The War at Sea*:

> It is only fair to mention that the captains of armed merchant raiders generally behaved with reasonable humanity towards the crews of intercepted ships, tried to avoid unnecessary loss of life and treated their prisoners tolerably.

However, he made one exception, the name mentioned being Reserve Lieutenant Commander Ruckteschell, whose story follows.

Reserve Lieutenant Commander Ruckteschell

Ruckteschell was given command of the raider ship *Widder*, official designation Ship 21, on 18 January 1940. He was 49 years old. Originally, the captain was to have been August Thiele but this arrangement was changed because of Hitler's strong feelings after hearing of the scuttling of the *Graf Spee*. This loss was an enormous blow to Hitler – very probably the power and strength of the ship embodied the power and virility of the new German state he had created. There was another naval ship called *Deutschland*. Hitler could not bear the idea that this ship, called after the country she served, might be destroyed, compounding the despair he felt after the loss of the *Graf Spee*. He therefore renamed the *Deutschland* as the *Lutzow*, and appointed Thiele as the captain. (This episode is described in W.L. Shirer's noted book *Rise and Fall of the Third Reich*.) This change left the post of commander of the *Widder* vacant, and Ruckteschell benefited.

It should be noted that Ruckteschell was already 49, and a veteran of the First World War, when he had served at Jutland before transferring into one of the early U-boats. He was later accused by the Allies of 'breaches of the custom of war' (namely war crimes). He was not brought to trial, but disappeared after the conflict ended, and went to Lapland, where he worked as a lumberjack, presumably to keep out of the way of the vengeful victors.

He returned to Germany in 1939 and was recalled to the navy. He was the only reserve captain to be honoured with an active command. It is possible, but far from certain, that he had a reputation for ruthlessness which encouraged the Nazis to put him in a job where ruthlessness was obviously an advantage from the practical point of view.

He was far from being a perfect commander. He suffered from the ailments which are traditionally associated with the submarine service. He suffered from stomachache and migraine headaches, presumably caused by nervous stress, and showed an emotional approach to problems. He did not have a good rapport with his officers, and no relationship at all with his crew. He stood apart, a lone, temperamental authority figure. His only virtue was a single-minded concentration on success in his command; but of course this determination led him to disregard any considerations which might impede that success, including any thought of decency towards the enemy. (Note, however, the comment later based on the contents of his log.)

He started as he was to go on. Shortly after leaving Kiel he attacked the British tanker *British Petrol*, subduing her with great violence even though she had sent no radio warning. He made the excuse that he had 'thought she would certainly radio and fight back', but what gave him this idea is unknown. Shortly afterwards, he indulged in similar conduct with the *Davisian* of the Harrison Line, again without any provocation on the part of his victim. The evidence of this attack was crucial in ensuring the conviction of Ruckteschell, after the war, on war crimes charges. At the time, it went unnoticed. The fact was that the British public knew very little of this aspect of the war, except in a few scattered reports. (*Sunday Chronicle*, November 1940, *Sunday Pictorial*, November 1940, *Newcastle Evening Chronicle*, November 1940, *John Bull* August 1941.)

The *Widder* continued her cruise north of the equator, and Ruckteschell worked out a consistent plan of attack, which he used time after time. He would mark out and stalk his victims until nightfall, when he would close in on them and smother them with 5.9-inch shells and rake cannon-fire along their decks. He said that this was necessary (without a preliminary call to surrender) to ensure that the guns were put out of action. In fact, each ship carried only one gun, served by one professional gunner, as was the case on the *Anglo Saxon*. Sometimes the gunner had five amateur helpers assigned to him – although no mention of these has been made by the *Anglo Saxon*'s survivors. This limit of only one gun was made necessary by British obedience to an old law of war, forgotten by many, a point reported by *John Bull* in an article on 11 January 1941. Only the British observed it, and they only breached it when anti-aircraft guns became a necessary part of each ship's equipment.

Ruckteschell also said that he generally targeted his prey by means of a door opened carelessly or a window left uncurtained. The blackout was strictly implemented on British ships by sailors who knew their security depended on it. It is most unlikely that it was so often breached, and may indicate a somewhat casual attitude to the truth on Ruckteschell's part.

It may seem strange that the victims did not notice they were shadowed in this way. But what were they to think? The raiders were designed to look like merchant ships – and if the victims thought of the matter at all, they would take the vessel to be another merchant ship steering the same course as themselves. Thus all the *Widder* had to do was to speed up and fall upon the merchant ship under cover of darkness.

The *Widder* did a great deal of damage and was able to view her voyage as a success until towards the end of 1940, in early autumn, when she suffered a number of misfortunes. The crew, who seemed to be traditional superstitious seamen, were dismayed when a propeller

The ill-fated Anglo Saxon

blade broke. Earlier, Ruckteschell had used the propeller to smash up an abandoned lifeboat, something that was viewed as inviting bad luck. These feelings became more intense when he attacked a Finnish sailing boat, an old-fashioned windjammer. Although Finland was not at war with Germany, the cargo and the ship's agent were British. The crew remembered the law of the sea, that steam gives way to sail, and regarded the act as criminal.

The rot seemed to have set in, a disciplinary rot which compounded more mechanical and seagoing difficulties, and Ruckteschell headed for home. He managed to get into Brest and drop anchor. He had destroyed ten ships and was greeted as a hero, receiving the Ritterkreuz (Iron Cross), the first raider to receive this honour. He was assigned to the *Michel* (Ship 28), and set sail again, to pursue what many writers have regarded as a successful but inglorious career, marked by further brutality.

It is only fair to say, however, that Ruckteschell held himself to have been unfairly victimized, and there is a certain amount of evidence to justify this. Here is an extract from his log, after the *Michel* and her launch, the *Esau*, sank the *March* on 27 December 1941.

> I recalled the launch. She had on board three prisoners taken in the course of the fighting. They were transferred to the *Michel*. In the meantime the launch received orders to look for and pick up any further survivors before being hoisted back on board. The *Michel* also used the time to rescue survivors, the first officer directing operations.
>
> 23.42 hours. The launch returned with 11 more prisoners, five of them badly injured. Between then and 01.00 hours, more survivors were rescued from the water. The course over which the fighting had extended was retraced and boats and rafts examined. The crew numbered 58, of whom 25 have been rescued including the master, who is the only surviving officer. We have spent nearly two and a half hours on the rescue operations and intend to return to the scene of the sinking tomorrow to clear the area.

Unless this is a complete piece of fiction written by Ruckteschell to conceal his true persona, it seems that he may not have been the conscienceless monster he has often been thought. However, the matter remains something of a mystery – and it may be that he showed leniency when he thought he could safely do so.

Captain Kruder

A very notable raider exploit, perhaps the most extraordinary that was achieved, involved the *Pinguin* (Ship 33), which captured two Antarctic whaling fleets between 13 and 15 January 1941. This was accomplished in part by very good intelligence work. There were three Norwegian factory ships the *Ole Wegger*, *Thorshammer* and *Pelagos*, servicing a number of whalers. By listening to the radio messages exchanged between the factory ships and their home management, the *Pinguin* knew that they were expecting a tanker at any time to take away some of their oil.

At first, the name of the tanker was not known, but the Germans managed to intercept a message from one of the whalers to her mother ship, the *Ole Wegger*, asking whether the *Solglimt* could take mail back with her. From this, the Germans knew that the expected tanker was the Norwegian tanker *Solglimt*, of 12,000 tons. The Germans presumed she would call first on the *Thorshammer*, then the *Ole Wegger*, and then the *Pelagos*.

The *Pinguin*'s captain, Kruder, decided to begin by closing in on the *Ole Wegger* on 6 January. Conditions were suitable for concealment, for there was a heavy snowstorm, and the radio traffic between the Norwegians discussed the weather, which was so thick that some of the whales that had already been captured and marked by flags were being lost before they could be towed to the factory ships.

Kruder waited until he heard the *Solglimt* getting closer. She actually made for the *Ole Wegger*. Kruder waited until the two big ships were alongside each other, and therefore unmanoeuvrable, and approached to go in for the kill. As he did so, however, the lights of both ships were obscured by a sudden snowstorm. When this cleared, Kruder found that the *Pinguin* was very close to his target. Immediately he contacted both ships, warning them not to use their radios. No gun was fired, but prize crews were sent over, and the ships were secured without incident. Simultaneously, the *Pinguin* lost the use of one of her engines. A cylinder cover had cracked.

However, the *Pinguin* found herself in possession of the *Ole Wegger*, a 12,000-ton ship, which had on board 3,000 tons of whale oil and 5,500 tons of fuel. She had a crew of 190 and stores for 10 weeks. She also had three 4-inch guns on board for her own use, the others being intended for ships in the whaling fleet. The *Solglimt* was almost the same size, with 4,000 tons of whale oil aboard, with a crew of 60 men and 4,000 tons of fuel oil. Kruder also found papers on board which clearly showed the ships to be the property of the Royal Norwegian government in exile in England, and therefore to be lawful prizes.

Close by there were four whalers ships of about 300 tons each. There had been seven, but three of them took advantage of the *Pinguin*'s breakdown to escape. The *Pinguin* could not pursue them because of her engine failure. There was a natural fear that the escaped ships might give the alarm to the ship that Kruder intended to capture next, namely the *Thorshammer*. However, he rather cheekily radioed to the escapees, telling them to get on with their whaling, and that they would be paid for any catches.

In the meantime, Kruder decided to try to capture the *Pelagos*. To confuse the Norwegians (in case any of them managed to communicate with his prey) he steamed away from the

Pelagos's position, and only later steamed back towards her. She was trying to contact the *Solglimt* and the *Ole Wegger* by radio – and, of course, her efforts were in vain.

To go to the *Pelagos* Kruder had to pass around an icefield. As the *Pinguin* did so, her crew saw one of the whalers attached to the *Pelagos*. They were actually flagging up a whale they had caught. This worried Kruder, but in the event the whaler did not raise the alarm. The *Pinguin* moved closer to the *Pelagos*, which was hard at work. Five whalers were alongside her, transferring their catch. The *Pinguin* came next to the *Pelagos* as fast as she could, and was within 200 yards of her at midnight. One of the whalers was boarded and German sailors went aboard to capture the others, while the captain of the *Pelagos* was told to order his remaining whalers to return.

This was a very notable capture. The *Pelagos* was a ship of 12,000 tons, and had 9,500 tons of whale oil aboard and 800 tons of fuel. She held provisions for ten weeks and her seven whalers were boats of 250 to 300 tons. If they could be taken to Germany, they could be used for anti-submarine operations. The total capture was 36,000 tonnage of shipping (not including the 11 whalers), nearly 20,000 tons of whale oil and more than 10,000 tons of fuel oil.

Kruder had also hoped to capture the *Thorshammer*, but she proved elusive. No doubt one of the whalers had tipped her off. There remained the question of how to deal with his prizes. He came to the conclusion that the *Ole Wegger* was too conspicuous, being obviously a factory ship, and so could not get through the Royal Navy's blockade unobserved. The *Pelagos* and the *Solglimt* were sent home immediately, since they had enough fuel on board to steam right up from the Antarctic to the Arctic and return home via Greenland. Later, Kruder changed his mind and sent the *Ole Wegger* and the whalers home, with the exception of one, which was renamed *Adjutant* and made into an auxiliary minelayer. The whole episode was notable for being the greatest success of the raider ships – quite remarkable by any standards.

Kruder was an exceptional captain who did very well with an excellent ship and good crew. Unfortunately for him, however, he was eventually engaged by the British cruiser *Cornwall*, and after a brief action the *Pinguin* was sunk. Kruder and all but 60 of his crew went down with his ship, as did many of his prisoners, though 22 were picked up by the *Cornwall*.

14   The *Anglo Saxon* incident[*]

The raider ploughed her way through the North Atlantic chop intent on adding to her tally of merchantmen. Her quarry was the Liverpool-registered *Anglo Saxon*, bound from Newport to Bahia Blanco with a cargo of coal.

It was 8.20 p.m. on the evening of 21 August 1940, and the 5,596-ton tramp freighter was some 900 miles west south-west of the Canary Islands. She had been part of convoy OB (outward bound) 195, but in mid-Atlantic the convoy dispersed and she was heading south.

The freighter was proceeding on a south-westerly course and, as the evening light faded, the weather became warmer. The crew had just finished their evening meal and the eight bells (8 p.m.) signalled a change of watch. Two of the seamen, Roy Widdicombe and Robert Tapscott, were put on the same watch. (See appendix)

Just before the *Widder* struck, Widdicombe had glanced at the wheelhouse clock and saw it was 8.20 p.m., an hour and 40 minutes till the end of his watch. The first salvo from the raider hit the *Anglo Saxon*'s poop deck. It demolished the gun and killed everybody in the fo'c's'le.

There was a series of explosions. After that, Widdicombe left the wheel and went to look out to port. Seeing nothing, he went to starboard and saw a dark shape which was the raider, racing towards them obliquely and closing all the time. It was a mere 400 yards away, and constantly firing as it came. Widdicombe turned the wheel to port, trying to put as much distance as possible between his ship and the raider. All the time, a hail of bullets was pouring into the stern, raking up towards the bow.

The third mate ran down from the bridge, shouting to Widdicombe to port the helm, which he replied had already been done. Widdicombe believed that the enemy ship was now only 100 yards away and firing with every gun they had. The starboard lifeboat was on fire and the starboard jolly boat was a wreck. Widdicombe found the body of Captain Flynn lying against the bulwarks outside his quarters. He had been hit with machine gun fire as he dumped the ship's papers overboard.

---

[*]This chapter deals with an account of the British ship attacked by a raider, the destruction and death suffered, and an account of the aftermath. It also serves as a good example of the devastation of raider operations. This is also the story of two men who survived after a raider attack, lived to tell of it, and endured a remarkably long exposure in an open boat, which still stands as one of the most notable feats of survival at sea.

At that moment, the first mate and chief radio operator climbed the port ladder on to the bridge. The chief radio operator confirmed that the radio antennas had been shot away and there was therefore no hope of sending an SOS.

Widdicombe estimated that the attack had lasted only six minutes. The first mate returned to the bridge and told Widdicombe to assist him in launching the jolly boat. Eventually, after a hard struggle, the pair managed to lower the 18-foot boat onto the water.

The small boat was in a hazardous position and faced certain destruction from the *Anglo Saxon*'s propeller, which was still churning away, drawing the jolly boat closer to the stern and under the blazing poop. The easterly swell was pushing in the same direction. Somehow, Widdicombe and Tapscott managed to fend the boat off the side, and with two frantic shoves were clear of the propeller. The *Anglo Saxon* was completely ablaze, and the raider was closing in to finish her.

As the jolly boat slowly drifted away, Ruckteschell on the *Widder* ordered the *coup de grâce* with a torpedo before his vessel disappeared into the growing darkness. The *Widder*'s trail of destruction since entering the North Atlantic on 21 May 1940 included the sinking or capture of ten Allied merchantmen totalling 58,645 tonnes.

*****

The survivors of the terrible attack looked around themselves and the boat. They were obviously in a state of shock, and probably took little notice of the first mate's attempts at comforting words. The fact was that they were all experienced sea hands, and knew they were in a really dangerous plight.

That first morning, nobody thought about food and drink. The waves were not as vigorous as they had been, and the sun was warm, which helped. Nevertheless, there were several with serious injuries to consider – Pilcher's right leg had gone stiff, and his left was pulped. They were all surprised that he had actually helped to row them away from the raider – it was very courageous of him to do so in the circumstances. All they could do for him was to make a sling to keep his leg from moving around as the boat heaved over the waves.

Penny, the gunner, had a mangled right hip, and a bullet wound in his right forearm. They bolstered him against the rolling motion of the boat, which naturally caused him great pain by constantly pulling at his wounds. Morgan, the second cook, had a jagged tear just above his right ankle. In addition, his whole foot was bruised and he had a badly-injured hand.

Tapscott had four splinters of shrapnel in his back which were removed by the mate. Apart from that, his only injury was a broken tooth. However, the nerve was exposed and he was in a good deal of pain. Nevertheless, he was in better health than the three wounded men.

One of the first things the first mate, Hawkes the engineer, and Widdicombe did was to pull in the sea anchor, put up the small stubby mast into the hole in the thwarts and the bottom boards which held it firm, and put up the lugsail. There was a good breeze and they reckoned they were moving at about four knots travelling in a westerly or south-westerly direction.

The next thing was to check over the supplies they had on board. They found a sea anchor, a boat hook, six pairs of oars, a steering oar, an axe, two balers, a rope painter, the boat's canvas cover, the lugsail and a few ropes end. There was a locker under the seat with a compass and also a colza-oil lamp with a bucket to hold it. This was used for signalling in Morse. There were also a dozen red flares, a dozen matches in a water-tight container and a medical kit. There were three air-tight tanks built into the structure of the boat. One was in the bow and there was one on either side, in the middle of the boat, which was 18 feet long. These tanks were intended to preserve the buoyancy of the boat if the waves swamped it.

A central point of interest was the food – and there was not much of it. Three 6 lb tins of boiled mutton, 11 tins of condensed milk and 32 lbs of ship's biscuits, all encased in an air-tight tank. Behind this tank was a half-filled water breaker which was a keg in a cradle. It had a wide bung in the top and two long-handled ladles for scooping up the water.

The only one among them to bring any personal belongings was Sparks, the radio operator. He had a small attaché case with a few bits and pieces, including some tobacco. Although all the crew had cases packed none of them had had the chance to get to them. To compound their destitution, none of them, except (again) Sparks, had much clothing with them. The weather had been verging on tropical, and clothes had tended to be discarded. The mate looked over all these items, and then started to keep a log on the back of Sparks' timesheets, and also cut a notch in the port gunwale to record the first day.

The medical provisions were very basic and of little use. There was a bottle of iodine, two rolls of bandages, a packet of medical lint and a pair of scissors. Items that found an immediate use were several rubber finger covers which the mate put on as his fingers had been burned when sliding down the rope into the boat – they had become raw and very painful.

They set about treating Sparks (Pilcher) first by bathing his foot in sea water. However, it was in such a state, totally mangled and crushed, it was obvious that it could not be saved. It was incredible that he had pulled an oar while in that condition. Pilcher said that he could not feel any pain and was generally in control of himself. However, he did have the signs of fever and had lost a great deal of blood. Nothing was said, but they all probably realized that he was very unlikely to recover. Eventually they managed to sterilize the wounds of all the injured men and bound them up as best they could, and their patients settled down, and those who were able did their best to help, baling out the boat when necessary.

The men passed the time by talking about their experiences during the raider attack. They also tried to figure out what had happened to all their shipmates. Morgan told them that while he had been lying in bed listening to a small radio, a shell had passed right through his cabin and took the set with it!

Pilcher had been asleep when the first attack commenced. He had pulled on his clothes (and was thus better clad than the others), then snatched up his case and rushed up on deck. He found that the port and starboard lifeboats were damaged and on fire. Seeing the jolly boat being lowered, he rushed across and jumped in. How he came by his wounds, he could not remember.

Hawkes was also asleep when the attack began. His cabin was on the inside of the engineer's alleyway. This protected him, to some extent, from the raider's fire. On finding the lifeboats useless, he had dropped into the jolly boat when it passed his position, as Morgan had done.

The mate had been in his cabin and had immediately gone to the captain's quarters, looking for orders, only to find him dead. He assessed the situation, saw that the ship was lost, and that there were only a few of the crew left living. The attack had been so fierce that the damage was done very quickly – the whole thing had lasted perhaps ten minutes. This agreed with the experience of the rest of the men in the boat. Speculation about what had happened to their friends and comrades was brief, since that was what it was for the most part – speculation.

They quickly established a daily routine between themselves. The mate, as senior officer, looked after the water, doling out half a dipper to each man twice a day, at 6 a.m. and 6 p.m. He also handed out a ship's biscuit to each man in the evening. The fit men kept watches, and steered by the stars at night, when there was inadequate light to see the compass. The wounded men and the watch off-duty sheltered under the canvas boat cover, which had covered the boat and kept the rain out of it while it was on the *Anglo Saxon*. It kept them reasonably dry if nothing else.

The mate was right to ration the food and water so drastically, since they had no idea how long they were going to have subsist on these limited supplies. He drained a little condensed milk to each dipper of water, and the ration of ship's biscuit went down to half a biscuit twice a day. Outwardly, he was quite optimistic, but probably this was just to keep up the morale of the men. Quite rapidly, everyone became constipated – nothing was going in, and therefore there was nothing to pass out. They slept a good deal. The sea was fairly calm and the air was warm.

One night they sighted a ship to the stern of the boat. She was blacked out, but they could see the outline of the vessel, a darker patch in the gloom. The mate lit a flare and held it over his head. It spluttered and hissed, lighting up the boat and the surrounding waves with a red glare. When it burnt out and they sat and waited, as it was obvious that it had been seen by the watch on the ship. The flare died down, and they saw that the ship had turned and was coming back. The mate suspected that she was a German, from her build, and also thought that she might be another raider ship. She came opposite to them, and obviously the night watch was surveying them very intently, but suddenly, she picked up speed and made off, steering north-north-east.

It must have been a terrible disappointment. It was after this, perhaps partly as a morale-booster that a tin of mutton was opened and half the contents were shared by all seven. That picked up their spirits for a while, and the healthier ones talked, in an animated fashion, about their favourite meals and drinks.

They had now in the boat for several days. The sun was getting very hot, and the boat still needed baling, since she was leaking steadily but not seriously. The mate and the third engineer did what they could by way of medical attention for the wounded and the gunner's arm was re-bandaged.

Nobody was giving up the struggle to survive. The mate, the third engineer and Tapscott and Widdicombe all had dips in the sea, finding that the touch of sea water refreshed their bodies somewhat. However, they were careful not to drink any, although they longed to do so.

It was now 29 August; they had been eight days in the boat, and the lack of water was beginning to tell. Up to now, everyone had tried to maintain a cheerful disposition to help morale. However, the beginning of September marked the end of hope for the wounded, who were steadily growing worse.

This finish to hope was marked by a death. Pilcher died at 8 a.m. on Sunday 1 September. He had been in extreme pain, but never complained, and even apologized to the others for the terrible smell coming from his rotting foot. They had discussed amputating it, but nobody could bring themselves to do so. In fact, such an attempt would have probably been unlikely to succeed.

All the other men respected Pilcher deeply. Widdicombe remarked to Tapscott, 'A proper man if ever I saw one.'

Denny, the mate, stated 'Some felt sick' in a short note towards the end of the log he was writing. He could have said that he himself was very sick. The others noted that his face was livid, collapsed with pain, and his whole appearance was somehow lifeless. Perhaps his morale had begun to collapse with the death of Pilcher.

The men began to find difficulty in chewing their tiny ration of biscuit, since they lacked saliva. Penny was very quiet, lying in the bow, his life ebbing away. Morgan, who used to be very quiet, chattered and sang, but this sudden liveliness was, in fact, a sign of growing insanity. They thought that he had been drinking sea water, particularly during the night when nobody was awake to stop him. Tapscott himself also drank some sea water, in spite of the warnings he received, but he did not keep it up and so survived. Widdicombe suffered very badly with the heat and Tapscott sometimes had to relieve him at the steering when he became unable to function properly.

They encouraged Morgan to do some steering, but he did not know how and was too far gone to learn. His attempts were, in fact, dangerous, and the boat shipped water and nearly capsized. On the day of Pilcher's death they made little progress, and nobody had the energy to dip over the side. They just lay and suffered and tried to protect themselves from the sun with the boat cover, now getting much the worse for wear.

On the evening of 2 September, the mate made his last entry in his log. He actually laid down the case for better stocking of lifeboats with food and drink – they were all very aware of the very meagre provision which had been made for them.

The mate fell ill that night, so ill, in fact that he was too weak to stand up in the morning. They made a bed for him on one of the thwarts. In effect, he retired as commanding officer. While he had been active, everyone accepted his authority. Now an argument broke out between Widdicombe and the third engineer and they argued over who should be in command. The engineer said that he had officer status and should be the boss, but Widdicombe said that deck crew (of which he was one) always took precedence over the engine-room staff. He may also have been thinking of the fact that he held a second mate's ticket, though he had not been working as one. In any other circumstances it would have been a ridiculous storm in a teacup, but here it was taken seriously. In the end a compromise was reached. Widdicombe, it was agreed, would be sailing captain. Hawkes, however, would be in charge of the water and keep the log.

This led to another argument. Widdicombe wanted them all to have a full dipper of water per day while Hawkes, the engineer, and Tapscott argued that they should continue the rationing as the mate had run it. Widdicombe was a tough man, and he insisted, and in the end Tapscott and Hawkes realized that he would take the water by force if they did not agree. In spite of the privations he had suffered, he was still strong and they agreed for the sake of preserving some harmony.

Morgan was now upsetting them with his insane babbling and singing. Tapscott was in a kind of stupor with the heat, however he still preserved some optimism.

The water was giving out. Hawkes wrote up the log on 3 September and noted that they were now having the full dipper of water (a dipper contained an amount which was about half the average table glass), and in fact there would be one more ration left, after which the water would be at an end.

On 4 September, the survivors were in total agony from the heat of the sun. Eventually they agreed to have their last drink and set to measuring out the last precious drops of water.

This proved to be a completely compelling task, and they had no attention for anything else. They were so engaged in this that they did not notice that a small private tragedy was taking place; looking up in surprise as the boat suddenly yawed, they found that Penny, the gunner, had left the boat. They looked around for him, and saw him some way away. He was face down in the water, making no attempt to swim. He had, in fact, committed suicide. Nobody had the strength to rescue him. They discussed what he had done, and realized that they themselves might be brought to consider doing the same. What was ahead of them? More torture and misery, nothing more.

The third engineer, Hawkes, wrote up the log that day, an entry which was to be his last. He wrote down his belief that the raider ship had done what he did in order to kill any chance of any investigation of the sinking of the *Anglo Saxon*. He also said that he thought they were somewhere in the neighbourhood of the Leeward Islands.

When night came, there was relief from the heat of the sun. Unfortunately, the strength of every one of them was fading fast. Even moving about the boat or taking the tiller was difficult, though they did the best they could. They noted that Morgan was rather quieter than he had been. They had now endured 13 days in the heat, and the water and food were all gone.

Then there was a final blow. The rudder was carried away by a heavy wave and they then lost their power to control the boat. It was then that Tapscott and Widdicombe showed their initiative and resourcefulness, for they fitted the steering oar to use in place of the rudder and tried to keep the boat moving westwards.

The mate eventually roused himself, and said that he was going over the side, and asked if anyone would come with him. Morgan, though obviously depressed, refused to do so, as did Tapscott and Widdicombe. Hawkes, the engineer, said he would go with the mate. Although the other men were clinging to life, they did not dream of trying to restrain the two officers or argue them out of what they were going to do. Everyone regarded it as their decision.

The mate and Hawkes got ready to carry out their exit from the boat and the world. The mate gave his signet ring to Widdicombe, with instructions to give it to his mother if he himself survived. They shook hands all round. Hawkes had a moment of bitterness:

'To think,' he said, 'that I put in four years of training – to come to this.' Then he and the mate took off their coats. The last thing the mate did was to take Tapscott's hand and remind him to keep going west, and warned him not to allow the boat to be carried away south any further. Tapscott was very moved by this gesture of help from a man who would soon be dead.

The mate and the engineer then stood up on the thwarts. Tapscott could not bear to look, and turned his head away. There was a terrific splash, and when he looked over the boat's side, he could see the two men floating, seemingly clasped in each other's arms. The mate's hair was normally a very light yellow, but it had bleached white during their voyage in the boat. It was now very long and shaggy and floated out around its owner like a patch of seaweed. The survivors watched it, until it disappeared in the distance.

Strangely enough, the death of the two officers actually made Widdicombe more vigorous and active. His incredible determination to survive took a new lease of life, and he took over command of the little boat. He trimmed the sail, encouraged and rallied the flagging will of his two shipmates, and trimmed the sail. He also made an entry in the log. Perhaps he was inspired by the fact that he had a second mate's certificate – also he does seem to have had more stamina than the other two. Morgan, especially, was in a very bad way, and slipped from time to time into bursts of insanity, becoming hysterical.

They drifted on. The lugsail swelled with the easterly wind which pushed them slowly onwards. They put out a sea anchor (probably a bucket filled with water) at night to keep the boat stationary, since they found it impossible to keep night watches. Morgan grew worse and worse. When the breeze dropped, the heat was worse, and Morgan was now drinking a lot of sea water. They did not try to stop him, since he only used the night hours to drink it anyway, while they were asleep. He constantly cried, shouted and sang. This drove Widdicombe into a complete fury. Sometimes he shouted at Morgan, so forcefully that Morgan was affected by it and became quiet. As the day wore on, he became quieter and even began to speak fairly rationally. Seeing this, the other two gave him the steering oar and encouraged him to take his turn at steering once again.

However, no sooner had they dozed off than Widdicombe was wakened by the boat swinging wildly about. Morgan had made a mess of things and Widdicombe was so angry that, even in his weakened state, he went for Morgan, who was knocked overboard. Tapscott woke just in time to see Morgan going over the side. He leaned over the gunwale, grabbed Morgan's hair and desperately dragged him back into the boat. Widdicombe was crouching in the bottom of the boat – his fists were clenched, and he was as hysterical as Morgan had been earlier. The fact was that all of them were losing their reason.

Morgan babbled on. He sang, he shouted and he cried until even Tapscott, who was normally an even-tempered, cool sort of man, thought he would be driven crazy by the racket. Widdicombe's temper erupted again, and he threw the axe at Morgan. It missed and went into the sea. Tapscott was annoyed. He had planned to use the axe to open up one of the air tanks which maintained the boat's buoyancy, and try to collect rainwater in the tank – that is, if it rained. But he had no energy to quarrel with Widdicombe.

They went on sailing west and put out the sea anchor at sunset. Morgan's babbling and crying gave them no peace, though in the early morning he went into a coma. He groaned and mumbled, but was quieter.

The new day dawned and grew hotter. They expected rain, because they noticed the air was humid, but none came.

Morgan then gave them a complete shock. He stood up and for the first time for days he looked normal, and his voice was clear. 'I think I'll go down the street for a drink,' he said, walked up to the stern and stepped over the side into the sea. When they next saw him, his body was lifting and falling on the waves. They stared at it – there was nothing they could do. They were now the only survivors.

The fact was that the death was a relief. They were spared Morgan's endless babbling, which had put them under a lot of psychological pressure. He was, they thought, better off anyway, better perhaps than themselves. Their bodies were slowly drying out, they were extremely weak and subject to constant pain and cramps.

It grew hotter. They sheltered under the boat cover, which kept the rain out when the boat was on the davits aboard ship. They were at their last extremities and actually debated the matter of whether they, too, should go overboard and end it all. There is no doubt that Widdicombe's inflexible drive to survive put paid to that argument. He was determined to hang on, and Tapscott, always compliant, agreed to follow his lead.

Day followed day. At noon, when the heat of the sun was at its most extreme and most grinding, they were driven to drinking their own urine – what there was of it, for there was very little liquid left in their bodies. The suffering was constant. Tapscott suffered from an

Captain Flynn, Skipper of the ill fated Anglo Saxon   *First mate, Denny of the* Anglo Saxon

aching, burning throat, and to get some relief he drank some sea water. This made him sick, and then he continued with 'empty' vomiting which supplied no relief at all. He began to wonder whether it would not be a good idea to think of suicide once more.

As for Widdicombe, he was seized with cramp in his intestines and was laid out on the bottom of the boat. He would roll around clutching his belly, sometimes bellowing with rage and uttering hysterical oaths and imprecations.

Neither of them could sleep properly at night by this time. They existed in a perpetual state akin to a coma, and hardly noticed the passing of the days, though they still feared the arrival of the sun, now their chief enemy. However, they still managed to steer, though erratically, and put down the sea anchor when darkness fell.

Eventually, the wind sank to nothing, and the boat lost way. They were just tossing on an oily swell. The sun was relentless, as it always was, and they actually decided they had had enough. They would go over the side. Tapscott went first, and then Widdicombe followed, but the cool of the sea water revived him, and he managed to drag himself back on board. Tapscott decided that if Widdicombe was not going to die, neither was he, and he came back on board too. Oddly enough, this was not out of friendship – but out of animosity. The ill feeling which had always lain between them had surfaced once more, and they remained rivals.

Nature tantalized them – black clouds appeared on the horizon, and they hoped for rain, but it never materialized. Their tongues were now blackened and protruding from their mouths. Widdicombe once again found himself in violent pain and he said, 'Let's go'. Tapscott agreed to this second suicide attempt, though he felt rivalry towards Widdicombe, following his lead. Tapscott rolled out of the boat, but automatically floated, drifting a few feet from the boat. (He had always been a good swimmer.)

He looked back to find Widdicombe clinging to the lifeline around the boat. Tapscott cried out to him, but Widdicombe did not answer. Tapscott swam back, and was amazed that he could still swim so well. He said to Widdicombe, 'Why don't you let go?' Widdicombe just shook his head. He was refreshed by the dip and found that he still had a reserve of strength, and Tapscott felt the same. They crawled back onto the boat and sheltered under the boat cover. There was nothing else to do since there was no wind, and the boat could not be steered.

Later that day, the heat was once again unendurable, and Tapscott had the idea of drinking the liquid in which the compass floated. They knew it was not water, but it was not salty and therefore should be drinkable. They had discussed the idea before but had abandoned it, since they felt it might impair the compass, which was so necessary to them. In the end, they opened the compass and carefully divided the liquid. They had about three-quarters of a table-glass each. They replaced it with sea water, of which they had a plentiful supply.

They got a surprise when they began to drink – a surprise which was a pleasurable one, at least at the time. They found the compass fluid was raw alcohol, and soon they began to get drunk, and started laughing and joking, their normal reserve about each other forgotten. It was certainly a psychological boost – they forgot their aches and pains and at last fell asleep, enjoying the first full slumber they had had since their ordeal began.

Six hours later, they awoke – with a hangover apiece. The air was thick and heavy and very dark, with no sign of the moon or the stars. They managed to put out the sea anchor and slept once more, to be awakened by a tropical storm. A few drops of water fell on the boat, and a puddle began to form on the boat cover. To their vast disappointment, they found that it was as salt as the sea water. The canvas of the boat cover was impregnated with salt from the spray which constantly fell on it, and this leached out into the water. They threw it over the side, and waited for the hollow to fill up again, and did, in fact, manage to collect a few drinkable mouthfuls. Then the shower ceased.

However, the air was still humid, and they hoped for more rain. This time they were not disappointed. Before dawn, there was a cloudburst. The rain fell heavily, soaking them and their clothes and almost filling the boat with fresh water. The first shower had washed the salt out of the boat cover, so it could be used to collect the water which was falling. They drank as much as they could, until it overflowed from their mouths. Tapscott drank three canfuls, and was actually sick on pure water. After that, he took the water in sips, savouring it like wine, and it stayed down.

They set to work to store as much of the water as they could. They took one of the buoyancy tanks from its fitting and made a hole in it with the boat hook, which was not difficult since the tank was made of soft copper. They were handy men, used to improvising, and they fashioned a set of runnels in the boat cover from which the water ran into the tank. They managed to store about six gallons, and then made a meal of the ship's biscuits which they had found so unchewable, having soaked them in more water.

They were now in their 23rd day in the boat. Widdicombe made a brief but informative entry in the log on 12 September which lays out their state at the time. The water they had acquired from the storm greatly improved their physical condition, which was just as well, because the sun felt hotter than ever before, and the sea changed its character. The water was more blue in colour and they passed floating seaweed. They remembered that the mate had mentioned the possibility of passing through a major shipping lane, and their spirits rose.

The sun was more of a problem now, though it is not clear whether it was actually hotter or that they were now healthier and noticed it more. They dealt with this by pouring water over each other, and shortened the time which each spent at the steering oar, relieving each other at frequent intervals. When not on duty, they always sheltered under the boat cover. They did not ration the water, because they now felt sure of collecting more. There was still plenty of ship's biscuit, which they softened with water.

The heat was terrible, and it was obvious that they were heading further into the Caribbean area where storms were frequent. On 18 September the wind died out completely, and they found themselves drifting for two days. They also, in spite of their optimism, ran out of water. Once again, they suffered the dryness which throttled them, closing their throats to food.

On 20 September they were rescued by another storm. They rigged the cover and went through the routine of collecting water once again. Then they soaked six biscuits and ate them. The biscuits were getting low now, but their bowel function had returned. After this they agreed to ration themselves to one biscuit a day, but still drank all the water they required.

They felt so optimistic that they actually did not bother to sail on the first night of the rain, because they felt sure they were now near land. (In fact, this was not true.) On 24 September, Widdicombe made an entry in the log – the last one he made. They were still maintaining the routine of watches and general ship-keeping which they had set up. They were also given hope by another heavy shower, which gave them more drinking water. Although they were intensely hungry, they consoled themselves with the thought that they would soon be on land – perhaps in only a couple of days.

In fact, they were to be at sea for another five weeks, five more weeks of suffering, of hunger, of thirst, and never-ending scorching by the sun. Increasingly, they existed in a semi-coma. The fact that they were much better off for water meant that they were conscious of constant hunger, while before, when they had little to drink, their appetite was greatly reduced. The days were monotonous, and could only be distinguished if something particularly memorable happened. Tapscott harvested some seaweed floating in the sea and rinsed it with fresh water. They found it was just edible, though it required endless chewing. Still, it was better than nothing.

On one of these monotonous mornings, Tapscott was dozing during the last half-hour of his watch. The boat seemed to have stopped moving and he wondered whether they had run aground. They had – but not on a beach. The bow was cocked up and the bow had stopped. Widdicombe was asleep. Tapscott investigated, and suddenly the boat stirred and moved, the water heaved, and about 20 feet away a great fluked tail broke the water. They had run aground on a whale. When Widdicombe woke, he was very sceptical, and wondered if Tapscott had gone mad. Tapscott was sulky at being disbelieved, and said that he knew a whale when he saw one.

It was now Widdicombe's watch, and Tapscott went under the boat cover. While lying there, he heard a thud against the sail, followed by another thud on the boat cover itself. Tapscott thought he knew what it was, and he was right. A flying fish had 'flown' onto board. He found it, after a search, wedged between two battens in the bottom of the boat. He had the head end, and Widdicombe the tail, eating every scrap of the creature.

It was tantalizing to find themselves now surrounded by fish. One day a school of whales appeared and swam alongside the boat for a while. This made both men nervous, being aware that the whales could be curious and investigate the boat, perhaps sinking it. However, the whales ignored them and soon moved on. There was one positive side to the encounter – Widdicombe apologized for doubting Tapscott about the incident of the boat grounding on one of the great ocean monsters.

Tapscott and Widdicombe tried to catch some of the smaller fish, but without success. Seaweed was getting ever more common, and some of the larger bunches contained tiny crabs and shellfish similar to winkles. They also tried making a fish hook out of a safety pin. It worked, but the metal was too weak, and straightened out when the weight of the fish pulled on it. They gave that up and concentrated on searching the seaweed, finding small shrimps as well as crabs and winkles. However, hours of work were needed to assemble even a small meal, and in the end they went back to chewing seaweed.

It was now 8 October. There had been squalls, and they had spent a lot of time sheltering under the boat cover. Once, Tapscott came out from under the cover to check the sea anchor, and saw a large steamer steering southerly. Widdicombe was asleep but Tapscott shook him awake. They pulled out the sea anchor and tried to row towards the ship. They tried whistling (the mate had a whistle), waved the oars aloft, and shouted despairingly, but all in vain. They would have been difficult to spot, and of course they were far too far away to be heard.

It was not surprising they made no more entries in the log. For the most part, there was absolutely nothing to record, and they were losing hope. After the passenger liner missed them, the weather was bad. There were squalls, showers of drenching rain (useful, of course, in that it replenished their supplies, but cold and dispiriting) and the increasingly heavy seas made baling necessary if they were not to sink.

They carried on automatically with the business of survival. As they were now in an area of hurricanes they were worried about encountering a one. The steering oar wore them out, and eventually they put out the sea anchor all the time, lashing spare oars to it to create more drag. It was essential to keep the bows of the boat pointing into the oncoming waves or they could be swamped. They did not try to sail – they lashed down the canvas boat cover and kept under it, thus managing to keep fairly dry and get some sleep.

It was probably after midnight when Tapscott woke up, pulled from sleep by the noise of the wind and the violent motion of the boat. (Widdicombe was a very sound sleeper, and was not disturbed.) Tapscott was immediately worried by the wildness of the sea, though the sea anchor and oars were keeping the boat's head into the wind. Water was beginning to fill the boat and Tapscott wakened Widdicombe. As he did so, a wave broke on the bows and water cascaded in. They had to work very hard at baling to ensure that the boat was not completely swamped.

Eventually they decided to run with the wind and the boat started moving. Every wave lifted them up, the mountainous waves crashed on behind them, and they slid down into a trough, only to rise again, on and on for hour after hour. All day this went on. There was no question of watches, for it took both of them to manage the steering oar. The waves were 30–40 feet high and they were moving fast – as Widdicombe said, they were making up for lost time.

Eventually, this violent weather abated – the waves were still rough, but they could rest. They took off their clothing and dried it, chewed some seaweed, drank a little water (slightly salty, but still drinkable) and relaxed. The air was warmer, and they felt better.

From then on, their dominant thought was food. They were ready to eat anything, even the peeling skin from their own bodies. They ate the little crabs they found in the seaweed and thought about food all the time, becoming light-headed, often sitting for hours with not a word spoken. They were too weak to stand, and pulled themselves around the boat on all fours. There was no more thought of keeping watches. Sometimes the boat moved slowly on the breeze, and just drifted when the breeze dropped. They passed seven whole days in this fashion.

Their mutual dislike resurfaced. They had just co-operated out of sheer necessity and Tapscott began to think that Widdicombe was manipulating him into doing all the work. He felt that Widdicombe asked to be relieved at the oar after only a few minutes of duty. In the end, this situation exploded. Tapscott punched Widdicombe on the jaw, alleging that Widdicombe had been about to strike him. He had suffered from Widdicombe's violent temper before so there may have been some truth in what he thought. It must have been rather a ridiculous conflict. They rolled about in the bottom of the boat, beating each other until Widdicombe said that he could not continue, and gave up as he was too weak. Widdicombe took the steering oar once again, while Tapscott kept a sharp eye on him.

After that, very few words passed between them, and the bad feeling was always there, although Tapscott did apologize for his action. From then on, the state of affairs was little better than an ill-natured truce.

Soon after that, there was a major development in their situation. One morning, just before sunrise, Tapscott thought he heard a fish strike the sail. When it became light, he began to look for it in the bottom of the boat and he was still searching when Widdicombe said simply, 'Look'.

When Tapscott got up, he saw land – a line of it stretching as far as they could see. They had been deceived before into imagining land ahead when all that was really there was low-lying cloud, but as they drifted nearer they saw it was definitely the genuine article – a coral reef with waves breaking on it. As they came nearer, they found a break in the reef and managed to guide the boat through it into the lagoon beyond. There was a sandy beach and patches of grass behind it.

Tapscott had not forgotten the fish – he searched for it, found it, and shared it with Widdicombe. They sailed on across the lagoon, avoiding shallow shoals, staring at the coloured corals clearly visible in the water. In 20 minutes, they found the beach and also found the strength to climb out onto the land. It was 30 October.

The first thing they did was lie down and rest under some bushes, which were well sheltered from the sun. At length, Widdicombe suggested they head north along the beach. He thought they should be able to find some people, as he reckoned that they had landed on the Leeward Islands. However, they found that walking was still very difficult. They were too weak, and collapsed after only 30 or 40 feet.

This was not surprising. They were both basically walking skeletons, skin and bone, with long wispy beards and hair. Their skin was black and shrivelled in appearance, with pustules and eruptions all over their bodies. They were in a truly awful state, having lived for 70 days in the most appalling conditions.

They just lay there in the bush – for how long they did not know. They were roused only by the sound of steel biting into wood. Some people were cutting through the bush and talking in English. It was a Mr and Mrs Lewis Johnson, who worked as farmers, and they were accompanied by several other local men. Tapscott and Widdicombe were unable to get up. They just lay there and replied to all the questions that were put to them. When they told their new acquaintances the date when the *Anglo Saxon* sank there was much surprise. It was then that Tapscott and Widdicombe, who were under the impression that they had been in the boat for 65 days, learnt that in fact they had survived for 70 days in those dreadful conditions.

Some of the men were suspicious at first, but when the log was produced everyone believed them, and the two sailors were treated with great compassion and kindness. The locals carried them out of the bush, for they could not walk. They were given fresh coconut milk, bully beef and some sweet biscuits. As a result, they began to feel very ill – so much food all at once was not good for people who had starved for so long. However, after a rest their rescuers took them to Governor's Harbour, the capital of Eleuthera, the long island where they had landed, and which was part of the Bahamas chain.

Though Tapscott and Widdicombe did not know it, the day after they landed in safety the *Widder*, which had sunk the *Anglo Saxon*, arrived in Brest, France. Ruckteschell and his crew were given an enormous welcome for their triumphant destruction of ten merchant ships.

After a short stay on Eleuthera, where Tapscott and Widdicombe were given the attention due to heroes, they were flown to Nassau. It was the first time that either of them had been on a plane. In the Bahamas General Hospital, the staff quickly took command and ministered to their needs.

They were suffering from exposure, starvation and prolonged thirst – the latter in spite of their luck with the rainwater. They were also suffering from pellagra – a deficiency disease which accounted for the shrivelled skin they both had. Their mental and nervous systems were badly damaged and they suffered turns of hysteria, depression and insomnia. Tapscott, especially, was so badly affected that there was doubt as to whether he would survive.

For eight days they were in isolation. Once this was past, their recovery started and their first visitors were the Duke and Duchess of Windsor. The Duke was then governor of the Bahamas, a wartime job which had been found for him in the wake of his abdication, and, it was said, because of his German sympathies. However, the novelty of the event was probably a tonic to the two men, although unfortunately there is no official record of this unique occasion.

A long hospital stay continued until their systems recovered. Widdicombe, in particular, was very keen to return to normal life and he eventually went to New York, where he was able to join the Furness Prince liner, *Siamese Prince*, which left New York on 3 February 1941. On 27 February the *New York Herald Tribune* reported that the *Siamese Prince* was torpedoed and sunk off Scotland on 18 February – there were no survivors.

One wonders whether Tapscott and Widdicombe's relationship improved after their ordeal but one suspects not, otherwise Widdicombe would not have been so anxious to leave both the hospital and his comrade in misfortune.

Tapscott took much longer to recover – he was far more affected physically than Widdicombe had been – which perhaps may be linked to Widdicombe's aggressive and active character. Tapscott eventually resumed his work in the merchant navy, and joined a ship at Montreal. He died in September 1963, at the comparatively young age of 42.

Of all the survivors, Denny – the first mate – comes out as the unsung hero of the whole affair. He tried to promote optimism, even though he must have known this was not altogether justified; he treated the wounded, especially Pilcher, as well as he could, doing everything possible to ameliorate their suffering. He enforced a more severe system of rationing which conserved supplies and may have helped the two survivors materially. Above all, despite his own suffering, he set a good example and tried to fulfil the duties of an officer, only giving up when he could no longer do so.

The whole exploit was a truly amazing feat in the history of the sea, and compares very favourably with Captain Bligh's famous voyage in an open boat after being set adrift by mutineers, although none of his 17 men were wounded, and he had ample supplies. (Thirty-two pounds of pork, 150 pounds of bread, 28 gallons of water, six quarts of rum, six bottles of wine, together with twine, canvas and cordage.) They never ran completely out of food or water, although they ran low at times. They landed at New Holland where they went ashore, collected oysters, berries and more water. On a landing at an unnamed island they captured 12 noddies (flightless birds resembling turkeys). Six days later they caught a booby (a sea bird), and two days later, a dolphin. Contrast this with the seven survivors, who were completely lacking in water after seven days, and only had dry ship's biscuit for rations.

As a postscript to the incident, it is worth mentioning the war crimes trial of Lieutenant Ruckteschell, which took place at Hamburg in 1947.

The evidence of the second officer of the *Davisian*, John M. Jolly, along with the evidence from the survivors of the *Beaulieu*, a Norwegian ship, seems to have been the mainspring of the guilty verdict. However, his treatment of the *Anglo Saxon* was linked with the failure to regard the safety of the survivors of the *Beaulieu* in the third section of the verdict.

Tapscott's evidence seems only to have influenced the guilty verdict by reason of the fact that Ruckteschell made no provision for the safety of the crew, by merely holding off and allowing them to get into the boat. It seems that no mention was made of the machine gunning of the survivors of the *Anglo Saxon* in the water.

Ruckteschell was held not guilty with regard to the shelling of the *Empire Dawn*, another of his victims, because it was said they 'offered resistance' and a merchant ship could not expect mercy if it attacked a warship. However, no evidence was given that her 4-inch gun or machine guns were in fact fired, and it is possible that the argument was a rather specious one. (This ship was sunk by Ruckteschell's second ship, the *Michel*.) However, that did not save Ruckteschell from a severe sentence – ten years' imprisonment which was reduced to seven by a confirming officer who refused to uphold the charge relating to the *Beaulieu*, a verdict which was handed down on 21 May 1947.

Ruckteschell seems to have died in prison, although there is some confusion about the date of his death. It probably occurred on 24 September 1948, but could have been in June of the same year.

It is worth noting that Muggenthaler, the American journalist, tried to justify Ruckteschell's actions by quoting another officer, whether German or British is not made clear, who regarded him as a 'Christian and a gentleman': a rather extraordinary comment given the verdict and his conduct. Muggenthaler also refers to the encounter with the *Anglo Saxon* as a 'battle' although all the evidence points out that it was nothing of the kind – it was a massacre, whether justified by necessity and the rules of war or not.

G. P. Jones' analogy of the voyage made by the ill-famed Captain Bligh of *Bounty* notoriety is an apt and illuminating comparison with the seven survivors from the *Anglo Saxon*.

Anyone who has read of that amazing voyage in an open lifeboat lasting 48 days from Tofoa in the South Pacific to Timor in the Dutch East Indies (3,618 miles) must have had to admire his leadership throughout the expedition and to some extent disregarded his previous inhumanity which caused the mutiny in the first place.

As an example of endurance that voyage was undoubtedly worthy of quoting but that undertaken by the seven survivors in their 18ft jolly boat, surpasses that of Bligh's, commendable as it was.

The following acknowledgement from the official account of the battle of the Atlantic highlights the recognition that Denny, Tapscott, Widdicombe and the other members of the crew worthily deserved.

> A debt we can never repay is due to the men of the Merchant navies, who, true to their fine tradition, and with steadfast courage, devotion and endurance, refused to be intimidated by the heavy toll of sinkings and the threat of their ships being blown to pieces in one of the stormiest oceans of the world.

15   The Harrison Line

The Harrison Line, which had its head office in Liverpool, was to suffer unique ill fortune during the Second World War. It was to lose no less than six of its ships to the German surface raiders, more than any other line. Here are the stories of several of those captures:

The *Scientist* comes to grief

The *Scientist*, another Harrison Line ship, was a sturdy vessel, a steel steamship with two decks, five holds, and a deep tank. She had two masts and was powered by a Bauer-Wach exhaust turbine made by David Rowan and Co. of Glasgow. She was launched in 1938 and cost the Harrison Line £192,330. She made a maiden voyage from Liverpool to Jamaica under Captain G. R. Windsor.

In 1940, she encountered the *Atlantis* under Kapitän zur See Bernhard Rogge, one of the most able of the German surface raiders. It was 3.20 p.m. on Friday, 3 May 1940.

His ship was disguised as the *Kasii Maru* of Japan, with her name spelt out in Roman lettering and also in a number of ideograms which looked like Japanese. (Rogge could not duplicate the name, since none of his crew knew Japanese, but he was fairly sure that nobody would be able to see through the disguise.) He was flying the Japanese flag, and the top quarter of his funnel was painted red with a white 'K' superimposed on it – the symbol of the Kokusai Kisen Line of Tokyo.

The *Scientist* was taken in completely. As the two ships closed, Rogge ordered the disguise to be dropped; the Japanese flag came down, and the flag of Hitler's Germany was raised. Flaps opened in the sides to reveal the powerful 5.9-inch guns. A smaller gun fired a warning shot across the bows, and the British ship was ordered to halt and not to use her radio.

In spite of the threat, *Scientist*'s radio officer, F. H. Compton, sent out a rapid cry for aid but after three transmissions this was jammed by the telegraphist on board the *Atlantis*. This broadcast prompted Rogge to open fire, and shells began to crash onto the *Scientist*, igniting fires in the cargo and severely wounding Compton in his arms and head. However, he managed to dump the secret code books over the side before staggering off to a lifeboat.

Very soon the *Scientist*'s boats were all in the water, heading for the *Atlantis*. There were some wounded, including one Asian seaman whose serious stomach wound was shortly to prove fatal. Some of the German crew came down into the boats and helped get the wounded secured to stretchers or wrapped up in hammocks and transferred to the deck of the German ship. From there, they witnessed the efforts of the *Atlantis* to finish off the *Scientist*. The Germans poured shells into her, but did not succeed in hitting her below the water line. In the end, a torpedo had to be used, which was a small victory, since the number of these weapons carried was limited.

The British crew watched in silence, desolate at the destruction of their floating home. One witness thought of his personal possessions; a hunting knife with a deerskin handle, won in childhood, a uniform bridge-coat in his wardrobe, two months' course notes for a qualification he had been studying for, family photographs. Everything was disappearing beneath the waves.

After this depressing experience, there was a small but pleasant surprise. When the captives were shown to their quarters they found them surprisingly pleasant. There were long tables, benches and basket chairs, the deck was carpeted with a number of mats and the lamps overhead had nicely painted shades. The facilities for sleeping and washing were also very good. The bunks were distinctly comfortable, with straw mattresses, pillows, blankets and sheets. These were for the white crew members, and Alec Watson, who seems to have been a conscientious chief officer, was worried about the welfare of the Asian crewmen. However, he was able to arrange to visit them under escort and found that their quarters were also very comfortable, and in no way inferior to those inhabited by the Europeans. This, of course, was entirely due to Captain Rogge's forethought and humanity; he had made sure that up to 200 prisoners could be comfortably accommodated on board his ship.

In fact, he tried to look after them in every possible way. Rogge's ADC, Leutnant zur See Ulrich Mohr, was appointed prisoners' liaison officer. He has been described as tall, scholarly and possessed of a genial manner. He also spoke very good English. He endeavoured in every way to win the friendship and trust of the captives. One gesture he immediately made was to install a loudspeaker in the prisoners' quarters. Music was played over this throughout the day, and there were also news broadcasts in English from the United States.

The prisoners had the same food as the German crew – although the Asian captives were allowed to have their own cooking arrangements, run by their own cooks, so they could enjoy rice and curried lamb. This latter became a favourite with the German crew as well. The German rations were received with mixed feelings by the English seamen. They were not very fond of the *ersatz* coffee, or the blood sausage and sauerkraut, but the meat, vegetables, soups, and dried fruit which the Germans provided went down very well. There was plenty of drinking water, which was sometimes flavoured with lime juice. Soap and water for washing were, however, strictly limited.

The Germans were also generous in their provision of opportunity for exercise. Two hours a day were allowed, but this was soon extended and sometimes the prisoners were allowed out for six or even eight hours a day.

Six weeks after the capture, the *Atlantis* made another capture, the *Tirrana*, a Norwegian motor ship. She carried wheat, wool, canned goods and army stores for the Australian army in the Middle East, also (as deck cargo) motor transport vehicles and field ambulances. There were 900 tons of diesel oil in her tanks, and she had not been damaged significantly when captured. At first she was looted and then manned with a prize crew while the *Atlantis* cruised on and made two further captures before meeting up with the *Tirrana* again.

It was decided to offload most of the prisoners onto her, and send her back with her valuable cargo to Germany. In the end 180 Asian seamen, all the original Norwegian crew of the *Tirrana*, all the British prisoners over the age of 50 (except the captured captains), all the boys under 16 years of age, and some of the sick and wounded whom Captain Rogge thought would be better off in a hospital in Europe were sent. In all, 25 men of the *Scientist*'s crew went with the *Tirrana*, including the chief engineer, Bob Scarrow; third engineer Dave Foulis; chief steward, Harry Howarth; quartermaster, Dick Barrow; 20 of the Asian seamen, and a Mr Chicken a passenger who had joined the ship at Durban. All of them left cheerfully – probably happy to be saying goodbye to the uncertainties of war with the prospect of a comfortable, if dull, imprisonment.

In fact, they were headed for tragedy. The commander of the *Tirrana*, Leutnant zur See Waldmann, decided it would be better that, instead of going to St Nazaire, he made for a port in unoccupied France. Accordingly, he headed for Arcachon and anchored off Cap Ferret on 2 September. The Vichy French authorities were not very helpful and made him sail on for Bordeaux arriving off the mouth of the Gironde the next morning. He had been warned that the mouth of the river was mined, and so waited for minesweeper escorts.

The *Tirrana* was cruising slowly to and fro when she was spotted by a British submarine, the *Tuna*. She knew nothing of the passengers, and only saw a large freighter loaded with military vehicles. She sent two torpedoes into the hapless ship, which sank very rapidly. Sixty innocent people perished. They included Bob Scarrow and Mr Chicken, the passenger from Durban. Dave Foulis and Harry Howarth survived, and lived out the rest of the war in German prison camps.

The prisoners who had stayed on the *Atlantis* were eventually transferred to the *Durmitor*, a very old Yugoslav tramp steamer, which had been captured on 22 October. It had been stripped clean and the prisoners had been shipped across from the *Atlantis* on 26 October.

The *Durmitor* eventually arrived on the coast of what was then Italian Somaliland, 28 days later. There was no response to their signals, and the master of the *Durmitor* tried to run her ashore on the reef which barred the offshore approaches. The ocean swell ground her against the reef and the old vessel began to break apart. The response was to ferry the prisoners ashore in waves, and this gave rise to local rumours that the Allies were effecting a landing. There were local colonial soldiers who were ready to fight and the situation was tense. In the end, the prisoners were marched away to Warshiek, a local village, and the situation was defused, otherwise there might have been a massacre.

The next day, the prisoners were taken off to a prison camp near Mogadiscio (now Mogadishu). The German guards were also kept in custody, although only until their credentials were checked. When the Germans were released, they commandeered a German merchant ship called the *Tannenfels*, which rejoined the *Atlantis* on 8 February 1941.

The war in East Africa was now winding down and the Italian forces were melting away. On 25 February the Italian guards deserted, and later in the day, a South African patrol car liberated the inmates. Three days later, the Royal Navy, in the shape of HMS *Ceres*, picked them up and deposited them down the coast at Mombasa. They were not prisoners of war any longer but DBS, distressed British seamen. It was mid-April before the men manged to hitch a ride to Mombasa on the troopship *Nea Hellas* (formerly the Anchor Line's *Tuscania*), she was commanded by Captain David W. Bone, a well-known author of the day. The prisoners rushed down to Kilindini Docks to stake a claim to a bunk in the six-berth cabins.

The voyage home was a lively one. At Durban, where the ship called in to refill its bunkers, the navy was looking for crews for a number of captured ships in the harbour. Most of the officers who formerly manned the *Scientist* transferred to a ship which had previously belonged to Vichy French and which seemed, as someone said, to be in 'good nick'. It was commanded by Alec Watson, formerly the chief officer of the *Scientist*, who sailed his new command back to England. The only former prisoners who continued as passengers on the *Nea Hellas* were the young cadets and the apprentices, the elderly masters and chief engineers among the former prisoners of war. They sailed back to Gibraltar in company with the aircraft carriers *Furious* and *Argus*, eventually reaching the Firth of Clyde. Some of the passengers had a rather heavy package of alcohol and tobacco in their baggage, but they were in luck, since the Customs men were on strike and they carried their contraband onshore unhindered.

However, there were a number of complications for many of the crew. These arose from the fact that the *Scientist* had been declared as having been lost with all hands by the Admiralty. As a consequence, the affairs of the seamen concerned had been wound up. Wages due had been passed to their wives, now notionally widowed, and the wives had applied for their pensions, which had been duly paid. In the case of apprentices, the 'premiums' that had been paid by their guardians and relatives to obtain them their posts, had been repaid to the relatives by their employers. Now, when the supposedly dead men turned up, pension money had to be repaid, and premiums handed over once more. All this was very trying, although no doubt the return of their relatives well compensated them for any problems.

The *Davisian* attack

The *Davisian* was on course for Barbados on 10 July, when the *Widder* was sighted bearing the disguise of a Swedish merchantman. Second Officer George Jolly had been carefully studying the intruder as she hove into view on a rapidly converging course. Two of her crew appeared to be relaxing on deck enjoying the afternoon sunshine. Within a half-hour the tranquility of the day was sharply interrupted by the loud report of a gun. The first salvo shattered the foredeck badly injuring the bosun, J. Poynter. The raider, rapidly closing in at a range of 3,000 yards, continued to fire on the helpless vessel. A series of flags depicting the international code signal 'STOP, DO NOT USE YOUR WIRELESS' seemed pointless under the circumstances as the aerials had already been destroyed in the merciless bombardment from the *Widder*'s 5.9-inch guns. Captain Tom Pearce rushed to the bridge at the first sound of gunfire. His vessel was now defenceless after his only weapon, a 4-inch gun, received a direct hit. The shell had seriously wounded the gun layer and most of his team. Wounded men lay strewn around the deck as the raider kept up her deadly fire power. Jolly was ordered to acknowledge the *Widder*'s signal as Chief Officer Alec Smart prepared the lifeboats. He then quickly amassed Admiralty code books and promptly slung them overboard in a weighted bag. Although he had complied with Rruckteschell's signals to stop and *Davisian*'s radio had been silenced, the raider continued with her relentless firing. It continued as the British crew in their two lifeboats pulled away from their stricken ship. The shelling and machine gunning only ceased when the lifeboats were seen making for the *Widder*. The injured were Second Engineer, J.L. McCulloch; Bosun, J. Poynter; Storekeeper, J. Davis; Gunner, J. Plimmer; and firemen, T. Lavelle and A. Lloyd. Lavelle was the most critical with a badly-wounded leg. The men were helped on board by the German crew using hammocks and stretchers.

It had been Ruckteschell's intention that the British crew, apart from those seriously injured, should be returned to their lifeboats and left to make for the West Indies on their own. It was only after vigorous protests from Captain Pearce that the German commander changed his mind. Only after the ship had been systematically looted and stripped of all its valuable equipment did Ruckteschell make preparation for its destruction. Charges were then placed at various points along the hull. Three violent explosions marked the end of the *Davisian* before she heeled over to port and sank.

Once all his prisoners had settled down amidst their new surroundings, Ruckteschell felt it was time to read the riot act. The Nazi commander left them in no doubt as to what he expected of them while in captivity. The following stark message was relayed to them via Captain Pearce:

> Captain – the war between my ship and yours is over! From today you and your crew are my prisoners! You will be treated here on board in exactly the same way as any other sailor. You will get here the same food as my crew. If you will obey the orders given, so, according to the circumstances, you will not have it bad. However, for every disobedience there will be only one punishment, and that is shooting! Please will you inform your officers and your crew about what I told you. I am going to give it to you in writing, so that you can repeat it to them
>
> I am sorry that five [sic] men have been wounded. They are human beings and soldiers and I feel sorry for them. My doctors will do their best for them and I hope that they will get them through. Later on, as soon as everything is settled, I will give you the opportunity to see the wounded. None of my crew is allowed to have any conversation with your men…also, none of your crew will be allowed to talk to my men! I repeat once more: there is only one punishment here on board, even for the slightest sort of disobedience the one which I told you already. The First Officer will let you know the hours in which you will be allowed on deck. Every conversation between officers and crew is forbidden! If necessary I will give you the opportunity of speaking to your crew from time to time.

Jolly has recorded that the prisoners' treatment aboard the raider was fair; that the food was plentiful, if the diet of sausage, gruel, black bread, synthetic tea and coffee was not entirely to their liking; but that exercise on deck was limited to a mere 20 minutes, morning and evening. Fireman Lavelle's health was causing great concern. His leg wound had become infected and gangrene had set in. Although the leg was amputated he died from his wounds on 27 July 1940. Next day at sunrise he was buried at sea with full honours. The ceremony included a unique monologue from von Ruckteschell:

> Comrades, Sailors. All medical skill and all carefulness could not prevent the loss of the life of this young man, whose mortal frame is lying in front of us. He died in consequence of the heavy wound which one of our shells inflicted on him. If the War shall have meaning, so it is necessary for us to look into his face with all awakedness, of which we are able to. We see, carved into his face, the great disress and pains and the destructions and the suffering and the misery which the peoples are doing to each other. And if this comrade, whom we are now giving the last honour, would not have done anything else in this world but that he has been waiting for this shell, in order to die here on board so we will thank him for his sacrifice, because he taught us anew to long for the peace. His soul is free and returned to its Creator. On the rays of the morning sun, far beyond the horizon, which is encircling us, our loving thoughts and wishes are following him with all friendliness into

his new empire. On this way, on which we are accompanying our comrade, we look into the divine sun and ask Her, the strength for peace to shine in our hearts. Then the death of our comrade will be a blessing for him and for us all. Yes, it is like that!

Captain Pearce, along with other survivors of the *Davisian*, became prisoners-of-war until the end of hostilities.

The Story of the *Tribesman*

It was realized quite early on in the war that the merchant shipping of England could not depend completely on the protection of the Royal Navy – they had to have their own weapons of defence. The guns which they received looked rather puny in the face of a powerful warship, but not every German ship was in that category. Many of the surface raiders' armament was such that an armed merchant ship could give a good account of itself, and that was exactly what happened on some occasions.

In the case of the *Tribesman*, the man appointed to oversee its defence was one F. R. Hill, the official gunnery officer on board. However, he was not a professional navy man. Hill was the second officer of the *Tribesman*, and was put forward for a rather hasty course of instruction in gunnery before being sent out to sea with instructions to carry out a practice shoot when she left Liverpool, as soon as the ship was clear of the Sandheads. (She was bound for Calcutta.) After sailing on 15 September 1939 Hill carried out this instruction.

The exercise was not altogether satisfactory, to say the least. The crew took up position round the gun. The breechblock was opened, and the shell, plus a red sack of cordite, was pushed inside. An empty oil drum had been dropped over the side to serve as a target. The breech was closed without trouble and the new gunnery officer called out the range and the bearing in the approved way. The sight-setters fiddled with the little wheels that altered the bearing of the gun, elevated it, and brought it round to the right bearing. Then the gun layer pulled the lanyard that fired the gun.

The resultant blast rocked the experienced crew. They were half-deafened, in spite of the crude lumps of cotton which served as ear-plugs. The docking telegraph was broken and everyone was covered with soot from the galley stovepipe. Insufficient warning of the drill had been given and a stream of seamen, clutching their belongings, appeared on deck – they thought the ship was sinking.

Everyone took some while to recover, after which there was a second try. This time, the gun jammed after firing. A young engineer who had in the past worked for Vickers Ordnance managed to clear it, but the gun was now listing over to port and it was decided, probably very wisely, that any further experiments should wait until an expert had looked at it. (In the light of later comment, it seemed that the deck had not been properly strengthened when the gun had been installed. The result had been that the deck plates had begun to buckle.)

When the *Tribesman* arrived at Colombo on 29 September, a naval expert was summoned to look at the weapon, which was an antiquated 4-inch Japanese gun dating from 1917. His report was very negative and a higher expert was called in, an engineer officer, whose attitude can only be called 'scathing'. He said that another round fired from the gun would have sent it and some of its crew over the side. After that the gun was remounted. When the *Tribesman* returned to London a genuine Royal Marine, Gunner A. Austin, was appointed to command it with the aid of a few of the ship's usual hands.

Twelve months later Gunner Austin found himself going into action. The *Tribesman* was attacked in December 1940, about 1,500 miles east of Dominica, at 15.00 N, 35.00 NW, by the *Admiral Scheer*, a German pocket battleship. She was sailing from Liverpool to Calcutta via the Cape of Good Hope and carrying a general cargo.

The time was 9 p.m. (21.00), and the German ship opened fire without any warning. Gunner Austin and his crew manned their gun immediately and opened fire. (Whether they would have done so if they had known what a formidable ship they were up against is not known. The *Admiral Scheer* mounted six ll-inch and eight 5.9-inch guns, and of course the *Tribesman*'s one gun was no match for that.)

There was, naturally, widespread panic on board. However, the radio officer, S.W. Lewis, sent out a distress signal. At first he did not realize that the main aerial had been destroyed. Realising his mistake, he used the emergency aerial, probably alerting the German gunners for immediately a 5.9-inch shell demolished the radio cabin – fortunately without killing anybody. However all the equipment was destroyed and there was nothing for it but to try and save themselves.

Bill Murray, the third radio officer, nearly left this too late. He went in to his cabin to save some personal possessions, and when he went to the boats he found that No. 2 lifeboat, to which he had been assigned, was already gone, as were Nos 1 and 4, while No. 3 was so damaged as to be effectively useless. However, he spotted a small group of men in the stern by the jolly boat. He hurried down there, and found that he had to go down a ladder to get into the boat, which was, by now, afloat alongside the ship. Descending this ladder was extremely difficult, for it was flung all over the place by the motion of the ship. When he reached the bottom, all he could do was to let go and jump, falling into the crowd of men who crammed the boat.

They knew at once that their only chance was to be taken prisoner. The freshwater canister had been smashed and the little jolly boat was very crowded. A few minutes later, a German launch hailed them and told them to pull over to the *Admiral Scheer*, which would take them aboard. Their fellow crew members were already climbing on board the German vessel from another lifeboat, and the jolly boat followed them.

They were naturally very depressed; their main worry being that the *Admiral Scheer* might meet a similar fate to that of the *Graf Spee*, and they might go to the bottom with her. In fact, they ended up in prison camps in Germany and survived. The lifeboats had got away (and there were at least two of these, with another 59 survivors) were never heard of again. They were commanded by two of the officers, Captain H.W.G. Philpott and his chief officer. No doubt the sailors aboard perished of hunger and thirst, but nothing certain is known. The prisoners on the *Admiral Scheer* did not know it, but they were lucky.

The ordeal of the *Craftsman*

The *Craftsman* was built in 1921. She was a fairly usual type of steel steamer, with three decks and six holds, boasting two goalpost-type masts. It was powered by two Brown-Curtiss steam turbines made by John Brown and Co. Ltd, of the Clydebank. They worked by single reduction to single screw which could drive the ship at 14 knots. Her cargo capacity was 580,310 cubic feet, and she was launched by the Furness Shipbuilding Co. Ltd, of Haverton Hill, Stockton-on-Tees, yard No 17. She was built for the Johnston Warren Lines of Liverpool, and was named the *Rowanmore*. On her maiden voyage she broke down 715 miles west of Bishop Rock on 20 May 1922. She managed to make Queenstown, made repairs and finished her voyage. She was passed from shipping line to shipping line after that, and eventually ended up (after five years swinging at anchor, laid-up) as the *Craftsman*. Her owners paid £46,152 for her.

On 9 April 1941 she was in the South Atlantic, sailing from Rosyth to Izmit via South Africa and Cape Town. Her position was some 800 miles west of Dakar, at 00.32N, 23.37W.

There was only one ship in sight, which was ahead of the *Craftsman*, off the starboard bow. It was apparently following a course very similar to her own. The two ships were passing each other, about a mile apart, when the stranger ran up the German swastika flag at the stern, and suddenly unmasked a whole battery of guns which opened fire at once. The *Craftsman* was repeatedly hit, and five of the crew were killed. Others, including the captain, were very badly injured. The captain, was in fact, blinded, and the chief officer, Mr Lewis, had to take command. He ordered the crew to abandon ship, and the badly-wounded captain was helped into a lifeboat. Only two of these were usable after the attack. There were other wounded men, among them Second Officer Ellis, who was helped by the third engineer, Dickie Profitt.

The *Craftsman* was a helpless wreck, and the boats pulled away from her. However, as they did so they were approached by a motor launch from the German ship, and the survivors were told by the officer in charge to row to the German ship. They were very reluctant to do so, but they had nowhere else to go. There were 43 survivors in all, and they soon found themselves prisoners-of-war.

A German demolition team went on board the *Craftsman* and planted charges to send her to the bottom. They failed, and in the end the Germans sacrificed one of their torpedoes to finish her off. She sank slowly. Her last position was 0.32N, 23.37W, 094 degrees and 349 miles away from St Paul's Rocks.

The prisoners found that the ship they were held on was a German merchant cruiser, the *Kormoran*, built in Kiel just before the outbreak of war. She had been named *Stiermark*, a liner of the Hapag Line, but now she was referred to by the Germans as 'Schiff 41' (Ship 41). She had sailed from Gotenhafen on 3 December 1940, and *Craftsman* was her seventh victim.

Three days later the *Kormoran* captured a Greek steamer, and the captain (Kapitän zur See Theodore Detmers) now had too many prisoners. In spite of 170 previously captured prisoners being unloaded onto a supply ship in February, the ship was very overcrowded.

Since he was also low on ammunition, food and other stores, it was decided to make a rendezvous with his supply ship. Point Andalusie, the site in question, was at 27S, 17W. When he arrived there on 20 April he found a small fleet. Firstly there was the *Atlantis*, another raider, the tanker *Nordmark* and the *Dresden*. The *Dresden* had come from the River Plate and was a blockade runner. There was also a British refrigerator ship which had been captured by the *Admiral Scheer*, one of Germany's pocket battleships, during the previous December.

Prisoners who were fit were transferred to the *Dresden*, but the wounded went to the *Nordmark*, because that ship had a very efficient ship's hospital on board. The *Dresden* was ordered by the German Naval Command to proceed to France, and eventually docked at St Jean de Luz. The *Nordmark* was sent to Germany, and the captain, who seemed to have been a very self-confident man, sailed directly through the English Channel. The prisoners on board actually had a tantalizing glimpse of England before being carried on to Germany.

When the *Nordmark* had berthed at Cuxhaven, at the mouth of the River Elbe, the prisoners were taken ashore and handed over to the Gestapo. After that they were separated. The badly-wounded captain was taken to a hospital. Second Officer Ellis was put in solitary confinement, and was subjected to repeated interrogation. To escape pressure, he told his captors that he had in fact been a bank clerk, pressed into service during the war. He said he did not know where the ship was bound, or what she had carried. To his amazement, they accepted this very unlikely story, even when he told them that he had been given minimal training, just a few weeks on a course on simple ship routines such as watch-keeping, elementary navigation and the rudiments of seamanship that was all. He said he was the third officer, not the second, and that only the captain and the chief officer took sights and read the charts.

It does seem incredible that this was accepted – especially as he was questioned by naval officers who should have realized that nobody would be given a responsible seagoing post with so little preparation. In the end, Ellis went to a prisoner-of-war camp at Sandbostel, in the eastern part of Germany. There was a small section of merchant navy personnel, an island in a vast camp which was mostly full of Russians. Camp conditions were very bad, not so much because of the actions of the Germans, but because there was a lot of disease, and there was an outbreak of cholera. This was made worse by the Russians, who hid the dead so they could go on collecting their rations.

Just at the beginning of winter, the seamen were taken from Sandbostel and put in a camp known as Marlag und Milag Nord, on Lüneberg heath (where the eventual surrender by Germany was signed). This was a special camp for merchant seamen, and Ellis and his comrades met, among the 3,000 prisoners, survivors of other ships of the Harrison Line, which had owned *Craftsman*. The Harrison Line lost no less than six ships, so their crews were well-represented at the camp. This place was a very different sort of experience to the first. The prisoners themselves saw to it that it was well-organized, and conditions were very much better. Ellis had been worried about the fate of his captain. Now he had some news of him, for early in 1942 a batch of prisoners arrived in the camp who had themselves been hospital patients, and who had been transferred after they recovered.

Ellis overheard one man talking to an acqaintance about having received good treatment himself, but that he had been sorry for the patients held in a convalescent hospital down the road, where conditions were very bad. One of the patients there was an older man, an English captain, who wandered about the wards sightlessly. Ellis at once made enquiries, and soon found that the captain in question was Captain Halloway from the *Craftsman*. He went at once to the senior British officer of the camp, told him about the story he had heard, and asked that the captain should be helped if at all possible. The senior British officer at once agreed, and went to the camp commandant. After several days of negotiation, a pass was issued to Ellis. The hospital in question was only a few kilometers away, and an armed escort marched with him down the road.

He was admitted to the hospital, and went in search of the blind British captain. He found him standing beside his bed, grasping the headrail. He was very pleased to hear an old friend's voice, and they chatted for an hour before Ellis's guards took him back. However, before he left, he promised that he would return, and said he would do his best to take the captain back with him to 'Mersey Chambers'. The captain was puzzled by this reference, but Ellis explained that it was the name which the Harrison seamen had given to their section of the camp, because 'Mersey Chambers' was the name of the Liverpool building which housed the Harrison Line's head office.

In the end Ellis kept this promise. The captain's health, apart from the loss of his eyesight, was good, and he was perfectly able to walk about. Ellis read out the letters which had reached the captain from home, via the Red Cross, and which he had never heard in detail. Another thing that Ellis was able to do for his captain was to contact St Dunstan's, the great institution which served the blind of the day, and get a large parcel of aids and information for him. This included a course in Braille, and a strange watch without a cover with raised hands and figures, which Captain Halloway quickly became able to use.

In the end, however, Captain Halloway was told that a prison camp was not the place for him. He would have to go to an institution for the blind. He was very reluctant to leave his friends, but one advantage was that he would then possibly be able to take advantage of the repatriation scheme for invalid prisoners-of-war. Eventually, that did happen, and on 26 October 1943 Captain Halloway reached Liverpool.

After the war, Ellis remained in touch with his old skipper, and attained his own command. Captain Halloway died on 9 December 1962, at the age of 82. Ellis exchanged Christmas cards with Halloway's wife, but the connection seemed severed. However, on the death of the captain's wife, Ellis received a letter from a solicitor. Enclosed was a cheque for £500, left to him by Halloway's wife, as a last token of thanks for his kindness. It was the last reminder of a strange adventure.

16   The most daring raider

This book would not be complete without an account of the most daring surface-raider exploit of all – and one of the most successful. This exploit also has an unexpected postscript, namely a story of death and disappearance to equal any of the late Agatha Christie's works.

The story begins with the capture of a British merchant navy ship by the man who was probably the most successful raider of them all – Bernhard Rogge. His prize was a very ordinary ship belonging to the Bank Line – the *Speybank*. (All the Bank Line ships had names ending in 'bank'.) She was of distinctive appearance, having a hull with a flush deck, with a short raised forecastle in her bows. There was no poop deck, and the only projections above deck level were two tall masts which supported aerials and derricks, and four Samson posts, that were set in two pairs, one in the stern, and one just behind the bridge. The funnel was cylindrical, and unusually high.

In fact, she was a typical Bank Line ship, and all these fittings were standard Bank Line fittings. She carried the Bank Line house flag (diagonal halves of red and blue crossed by a white stripe). Her funnel was painted buff with a black top, and the ventilators were buff with blue inside the cowls. Her hull was black above the water line, red below. When war came, she was fitted with a Japanese gun which had been made in 1917, and two rifles.

In January 1941 she was in the Eastern seas heading for Calcutta. She had a mixed cargo, but amongst it was a great deal of teak planking, and 100 tons of ilmenite. This was a mixed ore containing uranium and iron that was used to manufacture high-tensile steel. There was also a large consignment of monazite. This was a rare kind of earth containing thorium. Thorium was valuable in the production of X-ray and radio equipment. It was a very useful cargo at any time, and more so during wartime, when all these materials were scarce.

In spite of the value of the cargo, *Speybank* sailed by herself without the protection of a convoy. This was simply because the Royal Navy did not have enough cruisers to organize protection on a regular basis.

All went well until they were in the Indian Ocean, with Madagascar 600 miles to southward, when at 6.11 p.m. on 31 January she was spotted by a lookout on Rogge's ship *Atlantis*. Rogge immediately gave chase, and caught her at night. He fired warning shots and warned the *Speybank* not to use her wireless. In fact, only one serious shot was fired, when Rogge saw a British seaman running to the *Speybank*'s one antiquated gun. The man was Able-Seaman Bailey, the rating in charge of the gun, and the shell from the *Atlantis* knocked him unconscious, but did not kill him.

Shortly after that, German seamen came on board, and the *Speybank* became their prize. No doubt the crew expected to be made prisoners, after which their ship would be scuttled. However, this was not to be. Rogge had already been in trouble with his superiors after he had scuttled a tanker full of oil. This was not Rogge's fault. He had sailed with a number of spare officers and ratings who could man captured ships as prize crews. However he had been so successful that there were no prize crews left and the various prizes he had taken were left on board. His superiors had not understood this – but understandably, he did not want to have further quarrels with them. The *Speybank* carried valuable cargo which would be very welcome in Germany. He was determined to retain her – but who was to command her?

The answer was Paul Schneidewind, a seaman who had been trapped in Italian Somaliland by the outbreak of war. He had been aboard a ship called the *Tannenfels*, which was eventually ordered to leave Italian Somaliland and to make rendezvous with the *Atlantis*. Rogge immediately marked Schneidewind as the future captain of *Speybank*, but in the meantime he appointed him as second-in-command under a Leutnant Breuers. Schneidewind had, up until then, been a chief mate, and had to learn navy ways before he became a naval captain. The British crew of the *Speybank* was transferred to the *Tannenfels*, and the *Speybank* went out on scouting duties. (This was at the time when Rogge was operating with the *Admiral Scheer*.)

It was a time when suitable prey seemed to be in short supply. Rogge was anxious – the *Speybank* had to reserve 450 tons of oil for her voyage to Europe, and every day saw her fuel bunkers lighter. In the end, towards the end of March, he recalled Leutnant Breuers to the *Atlantis*, and Paul Schneidewind became the commander of the *Speybank*. He was delighted to have an independent command of his own in a very fine ship. He had 53 men; 12 Germans, 40 Indians, who were the deck crew and mechanics, and one British prisoner, the second engineer, whom he had retained.

He returned to Europe in style, sailing on the same course that Captain Morrow, the ship's former skipper, had planned, and he planned to react just as Captain Morrow would have done when sighted. The records of the voyage are missing, but it seems to have worked very well. He reached Bordeaux in 52 days. His arrival was kept very secret, with minimum publicity. The German naval command recognized that they had a unique opportunity and were determined not to waste it. The opportunity was simply this, that the *Speybank* looked exactly like her numerous sister ships – about 17 of them. She could go about the seas in a near-perfect disguise, impersonating one of the Bank 'family' of ships. She certainly was not going to be wasted on some mundane cargo-carrying task. Furthermore, Schneidewind, the captain who had brought her back to Europe, was the ideal commander – the daring and successful voyage home was proof of that.

So the *Speybank* was fitted out with her new role in mind. These preparations fascinated and alarmed the crew. Four radio sets were put on board with enough operators to maintain a watch on two sets at a time. Two quick-firing anti-aircraft guns were mounted on the bridge. Most ominous of all, large amounts of sand were brought on board to be flattened out in Nos 3 & 4 holds to form a new floor. Joists running across the ship were laid on top of the sand, and the final touch was a planking skin. After that, sets of rails were laid on top. There was speculation that they might be going to carry locomotives, but it was soon seen that the rails were too close together. After that, a large team of navy personnel came on board.

Eventually, their new cargo arrived, brought by a special train. It was a load of bulbous, horned spheres – mines. There was considerable alarm among the crew which Schneidewind had to take seriously. Firstly, they were concerned about the danger that the mines themselves presented. Secondly, and perhaps more seriously, they were concerned about their own legal position. They were civilians, but a mine-laying ship was a warship. They feared that if captured, they would lack the protection of a uniform and official combatant status and, in consequence, might be hanged as pirates by the Royal Navy. In strict terms of law, they were right.

The matter of the mines was dealt with by a simple explanation. Schneidewind assured all the men that the mines were perfectly safe if handled properly. The heavy explosive they contained was very stable, and required a heavy blow to set it off. If a mine was dropped, or even if a bullet was fired into it, it would not go off. The explosion would require a primer, which would explode when the time came. However, the primer itself was very safe, and if fire was set to it outside the mine case, it would merely burn fiercely. To operate properly, the primer had to be set off with a detonator. The detonator was sensitive, and could be set off with a hammer blow. But neither detonators nor primers would be fitted into the mines until they were laid. The mines were safe. The men were satisfied with this.

As for the second problem, he promised the men that he would solve this too, and later on, he did. He issued every man with an armband which read 'Deutsche Wehrmacht' (German Armed Forces) which neatly converted all the crew into official fighting personnel, and protected them from any possible piracy action. (It is unlikely that the Royal Navy would have taken this point, but it relieved the minds of the men. It also had the good effect that it left everybody's rank exactly as it had been before, and thus avoided a lot of reorganization.)

Schneidewind renamed the ship *Doggerbank*, but that was a name for private use. When she set out, she was to be known as *Levernbank*, another Bank Line boat. (For the purposes of this narrative, and to avoid confusion, *Speybank*'s original name will be used throughout.)

After a fairly long delay, the authorities gave the word for the *Speybank* to leave, which she did on 21 January, 1942. She sailed as the *Levernbank*, with signal flags appropriate to that ship and a copy of the British merchant shipping code book ready for use.

There were immediate problems caused by the architects who had supervised the fitting-out. When they ran into a storm, the mine deck began to buckle, and some of the mines threatened to break loose, straining alarmingly at the clips which held them in place. If they had done so, there would have been no question of them exploding, but they might well have dashed a hole in the ship's side, or at least caused so much damage that the *Speybank* would have had to put back to port.

The crew soon found that the problem was caused by the sand. When laid, it had been wet, and the sand had gathered into lumps. In between the lumps were air pockets. Now the violent motion of the ship was shaking up the sand and the air pockets were filling up, with the result that the sand floor was subsiding. If it had settled evenly there would have been no problem; but it had not, and a level deck could only be attained by first removing the mines and the wooden decking. This was obviously impossible while the storm raged.

Gruetzmacher, the navy man who was Schneidewind's right arm and second-in-command, called for all the rope that was available. A complex network of ties was set up, lashing each and every mine in place. It must have been terrifying work. The motion of the ship flung the men hither and thither, often dashing them against the mines. There was a constant threat that a man could be crushed by a mine rolling on top of him. However, it had to be done, and the men working unceasingly for hours until all was safe.

Eventually the storm passed, the U-boat which had escorted them thus far moved off on its own mission, and the *Speybank* sailed on down the Atlantic.

They had nearly reached the equator when an unexpected guest came aboard – it was Triton, god of the sea, decked with flowing seaweed hair and beard. He demanded that all persons who had never left the northern hemisphere before be paraded before Neptune and his court, and at noon the next day that came to pass.

All the inexperienced men whose travels had never taken them south before were ceremoniously shaved, tonsured and washed in sea water. The ceremony (which was much appreciated, even by the victims) was probably Schneidewind's idea. He was keenly conscious of the necessity of maintaining morale. If so, he succeeded admirably, and the *Speybank* crossed into the southern hemisphere with something of an air of festivity aboard.

On 23 February, about 450 miles north-east of Tristan da Cunha, the *Speybank* stopped, and the cover name of *Levernbank* was expunged from its side. Artifical rust patches were painted on, to make the ship look like a typical down-at-heel freighter. The ship was about to go into action, and the mechanics went down into the hold. Every mine was checked, and every tiny part was scrutinized. Then the primers and detonators were put in, although the mines were not fully live until it went into the water, and the 'sinker' fell away and switched on the electrical circuits which would enable the mine to explode.

They still did not know where the mines were going to be laid. However, there was a problem which would have to be solved – that of launching the mines into the sea. They had to be removed from the hold and tipped safely into the water, and it was far from obvious how this was to be done. At first, an arrangement was set up whereby derricks hoisted the mines up from the hold, after which they passed along rails from the hatch to the stern and a removable laying platform which projected out over the water.

This proved totally inadequate as the whole process took far too long. In practice, a mine had to be launched every 65 seconds while the ship was steaming at a speed of 7 knots. Under the trial process, the best speed they could achieve was one mine every two minutes – and this was in broad daylight and in perfect weather conditions. They came to the conclusion that when they started a mine-laying run, they would have to have the mines ready on deck before starting work.

The only problem was that to have mines ranged on deck, on rails, it would immediately betray them to any passing plane or ship. How were they to be camouflaged? In the end it was managed, and in a way that actually improved the ship's disguise. A long wooden tunnel was built on deck, running from No. 4 hatch to a point 20 feet away from the taffrail. It was long enough to accommodate 70 mines and wide enough for the handlers to work on the mines and push them forward under cover. When finished, the whole structure was covered in canvas and fake rope lashings, and large lettering proclaimed the contents to be the property of General Motors New York. In fact, the whole thing just looked like deck cargo, something which freighters like the *Speybank* regularly carried.

Eventually, the sealed orders were opened, and they found what the naval authorities had in mind for them. They were to mine Cape Town harbour. It was a port which Schneidewind knew well – and this knowledge was one of the main factors which had made the German navy give him the command. The plan was that the *Speybank* should lay short chains of mines across the mouth of the swept channel out of Cape Town. They were to be laid in a position which would normally be regarded as too deep for moored mines, about 100 fathoms. This would have the advantage that minesweeping to remove them would be very difficult. Another mine barrier was to be laid across the entrance to False Mouth Bay – which contained the major naval base of Simonstown.

What they should do when this was completed was conditional on their position when they finished the main job. If it was possible to continue, then they were ordered to lay mines on the Agulhas Bank. As its name suggested, this was a shallow area of sea, but an area of great shipping concentration. Virtually every ship passing between the Atlantic and Indian oceans used this passage. If it was disrupted, the effects could be very serious – scores of ships sometimes passed there every hour.

On 8 March the *Speybank* moved towards Cape Town. There was now the distinct possibility, indeed near-certainty, that they would have to face up to scrutiny and challenge as these were crowded seas. Schneidewind consulted Gruetzmacher as to how such challenges should be handled. Gruetzmacher's advice was simple – that the response should be sloppy. Merchant navy ships, of whatever nationality, seemed to have a hole in their head where signalling was concerned. Sometimes, even in wartime, they would not respond at all. When they did respond, it was invariably garbled and often incomprehensible. Gruetzmacher recommended that they fit in with this pattern.

However, the visual aspects were not neglected. The number of men on deck was restricted – the large crew the *Speybank* carried was way beyond any normal merchant ship's contingent. Nevertheless, there were always a few men lounging about on deck, as they would be if the ship as what it seemed. Gruetzmacher saw to it that they were always men who could be trusted to behave naturally and nonchalantly. He also selected men who were well-browned by the sun – for they could be taken for the Indian crewmen which so many British ships had among the crew. On the bridge, Schneidewind, Gruetzmacher and others were wearing the summer uniforms of British merchant navy officers.

Sure enough, at 4.30 p.m., they were visited by a plane which headed for them and dropped to a convenient height to make a close inspection of the ship. It signalled the ship with a light, flickering in Morse, asking for the ship's details. Schneidewind replied in person, taking a signal lamp up to the 'Monkey's Island', a small square platform on top of the wheelhouse.

The answer he sent was that the ship the airmen saw was the *Levernbank*, sailing from New York via Pernambuco to Cape Town. (He had decided to resume this *nom de guerre* now that they had reached a position which was consistent with the voyage he had assigned to his phantom identity.) However, he was careful to make the signals faltering and a number of letters were carefully miscoded. As was intended, the airmen could not understand it.

They came down closer, to get a better view, and saw the apparent Indians lolling in the sunshine, and received the cheerful waves of some white sailors. They also saw the 'General Motors New York' message on the false deck cargo. It all looked just right. However, they once again queried his identity. Schneidewind carefully garbled his reply again, but made sure that the 'bank' part of the name came through clearly. As he did so, the Red Ensign was hoisted by prearrangement. After that, Schneidewind waved his cap at the plane and calmly made off to his cabin. It was just right – the casual act of an experienced old sailor who was a bit contemptuous of all this faffing about by the young men of the Air Force.

They would have been surprised if they had known that Schneidewind was actually in despair, and certain that he had been detected. He wanted to leave immediately, steam away from the land and danger. Gruetzmacher and Langhinrichs, his assistant officers, had to exert all their powers of persuasion to turn him from this course. They pointed out that they could not go fast enough to escape anyway – and they repeated that they were virtually certain he had pulled it off.

Schneidewind was also worried that the airmen might report the ship's name, and that the real *Levernbank* would be discovered in some different part of the world, and the whole deception uncovered. Gruetzmacher's experience, as he told his senior officer, was that this was unlikely. The airmen probably would not bother to pass on the name, and even if they did, and the British authorities could not find the name on the list of expected ships, they would probably put down the whole thing to some bureaucratic mistake.

Eventually Schneidewind calmed down and they proceeded as planned. What gave him added impetus was the arrival of a signal from the German naval authorities saying that British naval vessels and the *Queen Mary* were expected in Cape Town. It emphasized that the minefields were vital – they had to be laid.

They proceeded – although they received a shock when they saw the lights of a vessel off the port bow. Schneidewind feared it was a patrol vessel and headed back out to sea. However, once the vessel was past the *Speybank* went back in again. At 10.10 p.m., everything was ready for laying the mines. Both ends of the tunnel had been opened and additional rails led from its mouth to the two temporary laying platforms bolted onto the stern. Soon the signal was given and the mines began to be laid.

As each mine dropped overboard it bobbed and floated, until a weight dropped away from the sinker and fell 20 feet through the water, pulling a wire behind it, which in turn pulled the sinker free. As the sinker fell away, it pulled a much heavier wire, which was the mooring wire. It also pulled the mine under the water, and when it reached the bottom, the tension on the mooring rope activated the mine's electrical circuits and the mine went 'live'.

Soon the first chain of mines was laid, and the ship went about to position the next one. There were six chains of mines in all, making the channel very dangerous to enter. There was supposed to be a last chain of mines off Simonstown but by the time the main job had been completed it was too late. Dawn was getting uncomfortably near, and the ship had to get away from its handiwork. The run was cancelled. However, the main job was well and thoroughly done. Schneidewind now had to lay the mines of Cape Agulhas. He set off to run past Simonstown and aimed to reach the Agulhas Bank just before nightfall.

He succeeded. The sun set at 6.16 p.m. and now that it was dark, the ship's company set to work. They had 15 mines still in the tunnel, the ones which should have been laid outside Simonstown. They needed 30 more, but of course they could not have been hoisted up in daylight. Now that work could be done, and at 6.30 p.m. they began taking up the mines from the hold. The laying platforms were bolted on.

Everything was ready for action when there was an alarm. A ship was spotted on the port bow, the laying platforms had to be removed, and the crowd of men on deck had to scurry below – their presence on deck would have aroused immediate suspicion if spotted. The quartermaster at the wheel was instructed to alter course slightly to carry the *Speybank* out of danger.

Worse was to come. The approaching ship made the signal NNJ, which was not contained in the code book at Schneidewind's disposal, and very soon it could be plainly seen that the strange ship was a cruiser, a warship. (In fact, it was HMS *Durban*, commanded by a Captain Cazalet. The signal was a new one, and meant 'Make your signal letters'. As usual, the warship wanted to know whom they were dealing with.) When no response was received by the *Durban*, there was no great reaction – they were very familiar with the sloppy ways of the merchant navy, and in fact at least a quarter of the ships they met did not respond to the new 'NNJ' signal. Captain Cazalet told the signalman to try again, this time in plain language, asking, 'What ship?'

Schneidewind now knew what was wanted, and replied '*Levernbank* from New York to Durban'. This reply worked. It was plausible, and heavy seas meant that an inspection visit to the freighter was impossible. Also, the Royal Navy was getting cautious. Only a few months earlier the Australian cruiser *Sydney*, a larger ship than the *Durban*, had been sunk by a German raider. Not only that, but the *Durban* was in need of repair and only one of her guns, the rearmost, was in working condition. Captain Cazalet was reluctant to risk his ship unless he was very sure of his ground. He asked the opinion of one of his officers who was an expert in identifying merchant ships. That man looked over the *Speybank*, which had every appearance of a Bank Line boat, and said that it looked as if the message had told the truth.

The *Durban* politely winked back 'Good night' to the disguised German ship and Schneidewind replied politely, wishing them a good voyage. The cruiser faded into the dark, and mine-laying operations recommenced. Everything was going well, the crew were happy and relaxed when an explosion sounded in their wake. It was almost certainly a defective mine, which was alarming in itself. But what if the cruiser heard the noise, and came back to investigate? The last mines in the tunnel were rapidly disposed of, and the *Speybank* fled to safety, heading further offshore.

Thirty mines were left to lay, but it was agreed that it would be too dangerous to lay them at once. They would have to return another day, with a new disguise. In the meantime, they needed a rest, and Schneidewind declared that the next day would be a holiday. The next morning, men with no watch to stand could sleep in. Later on, there were lots of men lounging about the deck, and breakfast was a cheerful meal for the officers in the captain's cabin.

All this was interrupted by another alarm. Once more, there was a ship on the port bow. Schneidewind went to investigate. A mast top was projecting above the horizon, probably about 25 miles away. It was a very tall mast, but thin, which meant it was probably not a warship – perhaps a large liner. He asked the engine-room for full speed, which was the usual reaction of a freighter meeting some unidentified stranger, and changed course to avoid whatever ship it was. He expected that the other ship would likely do the same.

He was disappointed. In fact, the newcomer turned towards the *Speybank*, an action which convinced Schneidewind that he was facing an armed merchant cruiser – a liner which would probably be armed with 6-inch guns, and powerful enough to sink the German ship. Schneidewind asked his engine-room crew to coax every possible knot of speed out of his engines, but in vain. The pursuing ship slowly climbed over the horizon, and had closed the gap between them to only 13 miles by 10.30 a.m.

Schneidewind was not ready to give up. He gave orders for a Red Ensign to be ready for hoisting, and the professional deck loungers got ready to display themselves on deck. However, he also got ready to scuttle and take to the boats, issuing all seamen with emergency rations. He prepared the radio operators to signal Berlin with news of their fate if discovered, but he also made arrangements for one operator to broadcast the signal which British merchant ships attacked by surface raiders sent, namely 'QQQQ'.

Then he pulled his master stroke. He gave orders that the *Speybank* should steam towards the newcomer. He was going to go on bluffing, and was really giving up very little advantage, since his ship could not possibly outrun its pursuer. Soon they could plainly see the details of the ship they were dealing with – and the two 6-inch guns she carried. The pursuer's signal lamp began to blink with the expected question, 'What ship?'

Schneidewind made an instant decision. He raised his signal lamp and sent a carefully clumsy reply. '*Inverbank* from Montevideo to Melbourne,' he sent. (He realized that his disguise as *Levernbank* might well have been penetrated, so now he became yet another of the Bank Line's many craft.)

The Germans could now see soldiers in khaki thronging the decks of the liner, curious to see the ship under interrogation. Some of them waved, and the professional deck-loungers, both 'Indians' and white men, dutifully waved back.

The liner was not yet satisfied – perhaps they could not read the clumsy signal. 'Where from?' they asked.

'Montevideo,' came Schneidewind's answer.

'Where bound?' came the further question.

'Melbourne,' replied Schneidewind.

There was an ominous pause. Then all tension was relaxed by the liner's reply, which was simply a friendly wish that the *Speybank* have a good voyage. Once again, Schneidewind sent a similar message in reply and the liner began to draw away. Once again, the German captain had tricked the British.

Two days later, a sinking ship outside Cape Town radioed for help, saying that she had been torpedoed by a submarine. Of course, she had not. She had hit one of the mines which Schneidewind had laid.

After this, Schneidewind was allowed to go back to Cape Agulhas and complete his mine-laying job. This was done uneventfully, except that, once again, a defective mine exploded as it was being laid – and another exploded for unknown reasons shortly after it had left the ship. These mines caused endless trouble for the South African Mine Clearance Force and havoc among a very large convoy, WS 18, which was then en route to South Africa from the Clyde.

It was after this that the *Speybank* made her way to Japan, taking some prisoners with her who had been captured by other raider ships. She had to jettison 55 of her mines, of the EMF type, because experiments in Germany had shown them to be seriously defective. She retained 54 torpedoes and 70 mines – mines of the T type.

On arrival at Java the Germans were welcomed enthusiastically by the Japanese. Their mine-laying activities had diverted British forces which could have menaced Japanese interests. The Germans were happy to go on holiday for a while. They left behind their prisoners and sailed for Yokohama after four days. The British prisoners found that the Japanese were far less easy to deal with than the Germans, and suffered a regime of very hard work and very slim rations.

Having arrived in Japan, Schneidewind was anxious to carry out more work for the German navy. He had just successfully managed a very daring mission, and longed for further glory. He proposed that he should lay mines in the Magellan Straits on the way home. His superiors did not agree – Germany needed raw materials which could only be obtained in Japan, and *Speybank* was needed to revert to her role as a cargo ship. Schneidewind was ordered to hand over the remaining mines to the Japanese, and the *Speybank* went into dock to have her special fittings stripped out. The holds began to fill up with such things as drums of vegetable oil. They also loaded tobacco for the Japanese forces in Saigon where they would take on rubber. At that time the Japanese controlled nearly all the world's supplies of natural rubber, something that was vital for the German war effort.

They left Yokohama on 17 December 1942 and proceeded immediately to Saigon, leaving there on 3 January 1943. Their journey across the Indian Ocean was entirely uneventful. After that, the German command had wanted to send him far south of Cape Agulhas. However, Schneidewind had the discretion to adapt the details of his orders. As captain and the man on the spot he was the best judge of what was needed. He decided to follow the route taken by British ships, near to Cape Agulhas – probably rightly, since to all intents and purposes he was a British ship. He was justified in his judgement, passing round the Cape without problems.

The *Speybank* now turned up the Atlantic, heading north on the last stage of her journey, crossing the equator on 26 February. It was just over a year since the boisterous, happy party which had marked the crossing of the line. It was here that he had to make a momentous decision.

On this return journey, there was one dominant date which Schneidewind had to observe. His orders stated clearly that he was not to cross the equator before 5 March. The reason for this was a simple one. When the disguised raiders sailed home the German navy had to ensure that they were not attacked by their own side – to all intents and purposes they were British or Allied merchant shipping, and legitimate targets. For this reason, when one of the raiders was one its way home, a Forbidden Zone was established by the German naval command. In the Forbidden Zone, no merchant shipping could be attacked, but Schneidewind was ahead of schedule. He had a choice – was he to waste time sailing aimlessly round the Canary Islands, thus giving his enemies another week to find him, or was he to risk going in early? If he did so, with luck he could be home within the week that he would otherwise spend waiting.

Schneidewind was a man who liked to get on with things, and he decided to go ahead and press on, sailing east of the Azores. He was about 1,000 miles west of the Canaries on 3 March when a vessel was sighted – a submarine. Schneidewind thought that it might be the escort home he was expecting to meet, and hoisted the recognition signal. Everything seemed to be in order. During the late afternoon the U-boat drew further off to port, and was lost to sight at 6 p.m., but later on that night she returned and fired three torpedoes, sinking the *Speybank* within a few minutes. She was a German U-boat, *U-43*, under Oberleutnant Joachim Schwantke – he had been convinced that the boat he had seen was a British merchantman. He surfaced, and he and his junior officer looked around at the wreckage they could see floating on the waves. There was the sound of a survivor calling for help – in what sounded like English. Since an incident in which American planes had bombed three U-boats trying to rescue Italian prisoners-of-war from the torpedoed British ship *Laconia*, Grossadmiral Doenitz had ordered that no survivors were to be rescued by German U-boats.

The jubilant crew of the *U-43* sailed away from the scene of their ghastly mistake. However, that was not the last that was heard of Captain Schneidewind and his crew. The whole business had a strange, tragic postscript virtually unique among the tales of the sea.

The Spanish tanker *Campoamor* was steaming into the Caribbean Sea, using the Martinique Channel on 29 March 1943. She was keeping within an invisible corridor between latitudes of 15° and 16° N. This was a route which had been agreed between the Western Allies and the Axis powers as a safe route for neutral ships.

Suddenly the bridge officer on watch caught sight of something afloat of his port bow. The captain was called, and decided to investigate. In some ways this was a courageous decision because the whole world was a war zone, and the strange object might hold danger. However, as the ship drew closer the Spanish saw that it was a boat – and not a lifeboat. It was rather like a punt in construction, and had a bedraggled sail hanging from an improvised mast. There was one emaciated survivor, one Fritz Kuert. He told a most amazing tale of the end of Captain Schneidewind of the ill-fated *Speybank*.

Kuert told this tale in several variations. Whether this was caused by the trauma of his physical condition is still not known. In the version published in the journal *Das Grüne Blatt*, he said that after the *Speybank* was sunk, only the punt, a raft, and a rubber dinghy survived. The rubber dinghy, which was a large craft, carried 74 men, including Captain Schneidewind and Lt. Fischer.

As the number of survivors decreased, those remaining grew more desperate, and the following is the account which Kuert gave of how the final end came:

> In a sudden squall the boat capsized and Tosen, Bergmann, Schapper, Cordes, Tillmann, Heller and Schuster were drowned. The rest clung to or sat on the boat and tried to keep it floating.
>
> 'Without a miracle we shan't last another night,' said Schneidewind. 'I'm going! How about you, Bosun?' The Captain took his pistol out of its watertight holster.
>
> 'No,' I cried and argued that we should live and hope but Schneidewind was determined.
>
> 'Shoot me first,' pleaded Stachnovski. Schneidewind aimed the pistol at Stachnowski's temple and pressed the trigger. The cartridge was damp and the gun misfired. Schneidewind pressed the trigger again and this time Stachnowski died.
>
> 'Not that way! I'll have a seaman's death!' shouted Binder, the seaman who as masthead look out had first sighted the submarine. He slid into the sea.
>
> 'Shoot me too!' pleaded the boy, Waldemaar Ring and the cook's mate Klockmann. Schneidewind shot them both. Only three men were left.
>
> 'Don't you go too, Karl,' I beseeched Boywitt, 'Nor you, Captain. With three of us only we can make the boat seaworthy. Hold on while there's still a chance.'
>
> 'No, Kuert, no more,' answered Schneidewind. 'When I'm dead, use my body as a sea anchor. Tow it behind the boat. It will keep you stern to sea. In a few days you should see the Southern Cross. Hold it so that it's ten degrees to port. If you make it through, let our families know.' Then Schneidewind shot himself.

Boywitt died a couple of days later, leaving Kuert the only survivor. When this news came out, there was furious argument about its accuracy, which was exacerbated by Kuert's changes of story. As for Karl Doenitz, the commander of the German navy, he and his officials did their best to ignore the whole business – the sinking of one German vessel by another was just too embarrassing. No doubt they cursed Kuert for being so stubbornly attached to life. If he had died, the whole matter would have remained a mystery for ever. It was a sad end for a gallant captain, who, whatever his ideology, carried out one of the most daring operations of the entire war.

17   *Other noted raiders*

The first successes of the surface raiders in the opening months of the Second World War convinced Admiral Raeder, the head of the German naval forces, to intensify this branch of the German war effort. The *Admiral Scheer* carried out a successful raiding operation in the south Atlantic, and by the spring of 1941 the *Scharnhorst* and the *Gneisenau* had carried out similar feats. Admiral Raeder now wanted to team these two ships with the *Bismarck* and the *Tirpitz* to make an invincible squadron which could roam the oceans at will. However, the *Scharnhorst* and the *Gneisenau* were still being refitted at Brest, and the *Tirpitz* was still in the Baltic. Hitler also had misgivings about this project.

Raeder was left with a much smaller mission, which would employ *Bismarck* and *Prinz Eugen* (the latter being a new heavy cruiser mounting 8-inch guns. The commander of this two-ship squadron, Vizeadmiral Günther Lütjens, wanted to wait for the other ships to become available, but Raeder ordered him to set out regardless. His orders were to attack merchant shipping in the North Atlantic. Battles with the Royal Navy were to be avoided. Lütjens' lack of enthusiasm for the mission was a serious problem, and had very bad effects. He set sail on 18 May 1941 and went out into the North Sea.

Intelligence reached the British and the Commander of the Home Fleet, Admiral Sir John Tovey, ordered increased patrols. Vice Admiral Wake-Walker headed a squadron of the heavy cruisers *Norfolk* and *Suffolk*. Also assigned to the operation was Vice Admiral Holland who had the battle cruisers *Prince of Wales* and *Hood* with five destroyers.

Lütjens was spotted at Bergen, topping up the *Bismarck*'s fuel tanks on 22 May. He then headed for the Denmark Strait, going north of Iceland. He had been advised to go into the North Atlantic between Iceland and the Faeroe Islands, but decided not to do so. Admiral Tovey had always thought *Bismarck* and *Prinz Eugen* were heading for the North Atlantic, and late on the evening of 22 May left Scapa Flow with the battleship *King George V*, six destroyers and *Victorious*, an aircraft carrier. This squadron was based at Gibraltar.

The *Suffolk* and *Norfolk* sighted *Bismarck* and followed her. At 5.50 p.m. on 24 May, Holland and his battle cruisers also came up with *Bismarck* and engaged her. The heavy seas hindered the proper operation of *Bismarck*'s range finders, but Holland's deployment of his ships was also at fault, which evened matters up somewhat. Then the *Prinz Eugen* fired a salvo which set alight a pile of rocket projectiles on *Hood*'s deck. Shortly after, the *Bismarck* fired the fifth salvo of its shells, hitting the deck of the *Hood*, which was lightly armoured. One of them penetrated a magazine and blew up. There was a terrible explosion, and *Hood* sank almost immediately. It was one of the worst disasters ever to befall the British navy.

The *Prince of Wales* had also been hit several times, and her captain broke off the fight, having had one of his main gun turrets disabled. Nonetheless, the *Bismarck* had been hit. One of the shells from the *Prince of Wales* had damaged a fuel tank. This resulted in a fuel leak and much of the oil stored in the forward tanks became inaccessible. It was decided that the *Bismarck* should go back to Brest for repairs, while the *Prinz Eugen* would go on commerce-raiding in the Atlantic.

Vice Admiral Wake-Walker and his squadron continued to stalk the *Bismarck*, while the Admiralty, stung by the loss of the *Hood*, sent large reinforcements – four battleships, two battle cruisers, two aircraft carriers, 12 cruisers and many destroyers.

While this effort was underway, the aircraft carrier *Victorious* sent out planes to try and further cripple *Bismarck*. The planes in question were Swordfish torpedo bombers, rather antiquated planes, which failed to make any hits at all. To compound that, at 3 p.m. on 25 May, Wake-Walker lost contact with the German ships, and for most of the day the Royal Navy had no idea of the *Bismarck*'s whereabouts or where she was heading. However, at 6.10 p.m. the codebreakers dealing with the so-called 'Enigma' traffic saw a signal to the Chief of Staff of the Luftwaffe that the *Bismarck* was going to Brest.

It looked very much as if *Bismarck* was going to get away because Tovey, with the main naval force looking for the German battleship, had thought that *Bismarck* was going back via the Denmark Strait and steaming in that direction. He was 150 miles away from the German, caught up in very bad weather with fuel running low.

However, *Bismarck* was also in trouble, mostly caused by human factors. Lütjens had sent a telegram to Germany saying that he would fight to the last shell, and this had caused crew morale to slump. Then, at 10.30 a.m. on 26 May, *Bismarck* was once again spotted by the Allies, in a plane (a Catalina) piloted by a British and an American, flying from a Northern Irish airfield. At first this sighting seemed to be too late. Their quarry was only 690 miles away from Brest and German air support would soon be able to reach her. However, the British decided to do what they could, and the antiquated Swordfish aircraft were sent to attack *Bismarck*. At first they failed, and nearly made the disastrous mistake of attacking the British cruiser *Sheffield*.

Bismarck could hardly manoeuvre at all. Her engineers had worked for hours, examining schemes for repair. The steering gears were useless and they thought it might be possible to blow off the rudders altogether with explosive charges and navigate using the propellers alone. But the weather conditions destroyed all hope of this. Since the *Prinz Eugen* had left, she could not help. She might have been able to tow the *Bismarck*, or act as a giant sea anchor, which might have enabled the *Bismarck* to steer to some extent. Nothing could be done, and during the night British destroyers went in with torpedoes. They failed, but the constant attacks wrought further havoc on German morale.

During the night, Admiral Tovey and his ships had been making all speed to reach the *Bismarck*, and they arrived with the daylight. *King George* and *Rodney* came in for the kill. *Bismarck* was limping along on an erratic course, and although she tried to turn so that her broadside could be brought to bear, it was a struggle. In fairness to Lütjens, he carried out his promise to fight to the end. But the truth was that he did not inflict any significant injury on the British ships and soon *Bismarck* was a ruin, her guns silent.

The only fly in the British ointment was that Admiral Tovey's command was now desperately short of fuel, and *Bismarck* was still afloat. Eventually she went to the bottom, although whether it was the heavy cruiser *Dorsetshire*'s torpedoes that did the job or German scuttling charges is not clear. Of her 2,200, crew 110 sank with her. If rescue attempts had not been cut short by a fear of U-boat attack, even those casualties might have been avoided. (The ship's cat was among the survivors.)

These were the last of the German raiders – the loss of the *Bismarck* convinced Hitler that this way of attacking was useless. *Scharnhorst*, *Gneisenau* and *Prinz Eugen* were recalled to Germany in February 1942. After that, the war of the Atlantic would be fought by the U-boats.

Raids on Ben Line steamers

Ben Line steamers, based in Leith, lost 14 ships by enemy action between 1940 and 1945. Two of them, the *Benarty 3* (1,960 tons) and the *Benavon* (9,600 tons) fell victim to Nazi surface raiders within the space of 24 hours.

Benarty 3 was in the Indian Ocean on 10 September 1940, when she was attacked by an aircraft from a raider, believed to have been the *Freinfels*. The British captain had sighted a vessel about five points abaft the port beam, steaming in the same direction and converging slightly. *Benarty* immediately altered course and came stern on to the other vessel, which soon disappeared. However, some 30 minutes later a single-seater seaplane was spotted which flew straight towards the British vessel. The steamer was machine gunned fore and aft for almost an hour. Although the *Benarty* fired four shots which fell short, the British vessel surrendered and the crew took to the boats.

The German boarding party took much loot from the captured vessel, including navigating instruments, clocks, radios, engine-room tools and the ship's bell. Rogge, the German captain, was very interested in the ship's dinghy. Apparently he was well-known in British and German yachting circles and wanted the dinghy for his own private use. After the systematic looting was completed, the raiders set time bombs and the vessel was blown up within 12 minutes.

The next day at around 6.25 a.m. the *Benavon*, homeward bound from Penang by way of South Africa, sighted a vessel which turned out to be the same raider that had accounted for her sister ship the previous day.

The following account is taken from the Ben Line records. Awakened by the sound of gunfire, Chief Engineer R.C. Porteous saw a ship lying across the stern of his vessel, some 500 yards away. Porteous hurried along the deck to see Captain Thomson, clad in pyjamas, on the bridge. Soon after, the ship was subject to a relentless bombardment. Although the engine-room was mainly undamaged the bunkers were hit several times. The *Benavon*, with her light armament, was fighting a one-sided contest. Although her gunners had hit a magazine on the enemy vessel, the shell had failed to explode.

Following an hour of almost continuous shelling, the ship became a blazing furnace. The lifeboats were blown away and the only remaining one was badly damaged. Porteous, along with the second engineer, Crawford, searched the ship for crew members. They found some of them assembled on the afterdeck close to the only remaining raft. Fearful that the nearby magazine would explode, they eventually succeeded in lowering the wounded onto the raft. The chief engineer, the second engineer and the boatswain took to the water and managed to steer the raft clear of the stricken vessel. However, the third engineer died in the water. According to the chief engineer's report, the German vessel stood idly by. It was not until an hour later that they had the humanity to lower a boat. Eventually all the survivors were taken aboard the raider, which bore the name *Trafalgar* and was painted in the colours of a well-known Norwegian shipping company.

Some of the survivors died on board the raider. The remaining seven British and 18 Chinese, all that remained of a crew of 50, became prisoners-of-war. After the *Benavon* was reported missing in September 1940 nothing was heard of the survivors until March 1941.

The *Benavon* was one of the few Allied vessels that had dared to stand up to a German raider but she had paid dearly for her actions. It is thought that the enemy ship had fired some 59 shells from her 5.9-inch guns, most of them hitting the British vessel. The ship's master, Captain Thomson, who was directing the survivors to abandon ship, and never left his bridge, was killed by one of the last shells.

HMS *Cornwall* sank the German raider in May 1941. Unfortunately a number of merchant seamen who were prisoners on board perished, but 28 were saved.

18 The *Graf Spee*

Although the larger and more famous of the Nazi raiders have been described elsewhere, no comprehensive account of the early naval struggle over commerce on the sea's surface would be complete without a mention of the role of the *Graf Spee.*

Captain Langsdorff received orders in late September, 1939 to start operations as a commerce raider. He was already far down in the South Atlantic, having been cruising quietly in out-of-the-way areas of the ocean until he received his orders. After this, he moved into the way of ships plying between Pernambuco, Brazil and Cape Town, and soon sank a British merchantman after transferring the crew to his own vessel. For the next few months, he attacked a number of vessels, disappearing after each attack until he had carried out nine successful sinkings. In the wider context of the Second World War, it would seem a pinprick, but it was taken very seriously by the Admiralty. In fact, a sizeable amount of British naval strength was assigned to the job: two aircraft carriers, one battle cruiser, four heavy cruisers, and two light cruisers – and that was just the British contribution! Ten Allied destroyers and two French heavy cruisers were added to the formidable squadron which was chasing the German vessel.

The *Graf Spee* was not an armed raider converted from a merchant ship, as were many of the regular warships, but a warship with 11-inch guns that could fire nearly 18 miles. She was powerful enough to make a mockery of the nickname 'pocket-battleship' which was accorded to her and her sister craft.

Shortly after sinking her ninth victim, she made a rendezvous with the supply ship *Altmark*. She took on fuel and got rid of more than 300 prisoners, which Captain Langsdorff obviously regarded as an encumbrance. Oddly enough, these prisoners changed the course of the war, when Churchill's rescue of them in Norwegian waters, in spite of Norwegian neutrality, prompted Hitler to invade Norway.

Graf Spee's First Victim

On 10 October 1939 the *Huntsman*, a four-masted freighter of over 8,000 tons, was in the South Atlantic and heading towards Freetown to link up with a homeward-bound convoy. She had left Colombo and touched Port Sudan on her return journey from Calcutta. Two days out from Suez, a patrolling cruiser signalled to her that because of U-boat threats, the

Mediterranean was closed to British shipping. Along with many other merchantmen she was re-routed around the Cape.

The Liverpool-based Harrison Line ship had a crew of 84 and was carrying a mixed cargo of Smyrna-type carpets, jute, tea and an assortment of tropical equipment. She had been at sea for almost 11 days and was two days south of the line about 08.30 S and 05.15 W. Most of the crew were about to have their tea on this pleasant, calm and sunny afternoon. Although the master, Captain A.H. Brown, conceded that they might hit some rough weather on the way home, this was something that he considered unlikely. Besides, the Royal Navy was patrolling the northern lane searching for the German vessel, *Scheer*.

Chief Officer Alfred Holt Thompson had handed over the watch to Third Officer Les Frost, who had come up to the bridge to relieve him for the evening meal. About halfway through the meal, Frost sent word to his superiors that he had sighted a menacing-looking dark silhouette on the horizon due east. Captain Brown was alerted and quickly made his way to the bridge with Thompson close at his heels. Peering through his binoculars, Brown spotted the French tricolour fluttering above the quarterdeck of the 'stranger'. Within seconds the tricolour had been hauled down and replaced by the swastika of Nazi Germany. Wireless Operator B. C. McCorry was immediately alerted about the 'mystery' vessel. A string of flags were hoisted up to her yardarm followed by another spelling out the signals 'Heave to' and 'Do not use your radio'. However, almost oblivious to what was happening around him, Radio Officer A. Taylor was already tapping out details of the raider's presence: RRRR GFWS-Huntsman-attacked by unknown warship-LAT 8 30 S-LONG 5 15 W approximately 195 degrees and 830 miles from Takoradi. Although Taylor continued to relay the message until Brown ordered him to stop, the urgent transmission was made during an off-watch period for single-operator ships during that early stage of the conflict so was not picked up.

Captain Brown had already complied with Langsdorff's instructions and instructed Thompson to dispose of the Admiralty code books over the side. In the space of a few minutes the *Graf Spee*'s boarding party, armed with weapons including hand grenades, was rounding up the startled *Huntsman* crew. Later, the 40-strong boarding party was replaced by a prize crew of 25 men under the command of a Leutnant zur See Schunemann. Fearful that the Britons were about to scuttle their ship, Schunemann, Luger pistol in hand, ordered Second Engineer Creer to stay put on the manoeuvring platform while his men disappeared below to check the engine-room.

Captain Brown duly received a receipt from Langsdorff confirming that the *Huntsman* and her cargo were now a prize and the lawful property of the German Reich. Determined to waste no time and anxious to depart from the scene of the action, *Graf Spee* proceeded on a south-westerly course, with the *Huntsman* following in her wake. On board their prize, the raiders stationed armed guards throughout the ship and placed machine guns at the bridge wings. The captured crew were under constant scrutiny but resumed their duties as best they could. The officers played no part in navigating and were denied access to charts.

Two days later *Graf Spee* signalled a halt. It was time for a break to consider matters. Now fully aware that his recent actions must have alerted the Royal Navy, Langsdorff summoned Schunemann from the *Huntsman* for an urgent consultation. Less than an hour later the prize officer was back on board the British vessel after a plan had been hatched for *Graf Spee* and her prize to rendezvous with the tanker *Altmark*. The ships met as arranged and launches shuttled between them ferrying cargo to and fro. In an orderly and efficient display of Teutonic planning the *Huntsman* was relieved of her valuable cargo. Nothing was overlooked from her high quality Indian carpets to chests of tea and electrical fittings The crew were ordered to collect all their personal effects before being lined up on deck for inspection by their German masters. They were then ferried across to the waiting 'prison ship'. In keeping with strict naval tradition, Captain Brown was the last man to leave his ill-fated ship. Within a few minutes a launch carrying a demolition squad eased alongside the vessel to place charges below her water line. Apart from damage to her port side, the ship was not submitting to the elements. Further explosives were needed before she disappeared below the waves.

This was the end of five ships belonging to the Harrison Line, and just one of *Graf Spee*'s many victims. One of the so-called 'pocket' battleships which were built by Germany under the Treaty of Versailles which restricted its naval strength, the *Graf Spee* was an ideal commerce raider. When war broke out, she went to work, sinking nine ships in just over two months. This resulted in Captain Langsdorff and his ship being placed at the top of the Allies' 'most wanted' list.

However, in the very last days of November, a squadron commander called Henry Harwood made a breakthrough. He had been studying the pattern of sinkings by the *Graf Spee* plotted on his charts. He came to believe that the German ship he was seeking was going in the direction of the shipping lanes leading to Buenos Aires and Montevideo. He radioed his squadron and told them to move towards Montevideo at the mouth of the River Plate and to arrive by 12 December. He chose that date because he expected the *Graf Spee* to arrive. Harwood commanded two heavy and two light cruisers, but it happened that one of the heavy cruisers was undergoing a refit in the Falkland Islands, and could not leave for another day.

This posed a serious problem, since it deprived Harwood of much of his firepower. The *Exeter*, his heavy cruiser, mounted six 8-inch guns, while the two light cruisers, including the *Achilles*, mounted eight 6-inch guns each. The *Graf Spee* was much more powerful in spite of her modest size. She boasted six 11-inch guns and eight 5.9-inch guns, so that one broadside threw more weight of metal against the British ships than all their guns combined. Not only that, but the *Graf Spee*'s guns had a range of nearly 18 miles, while the British guns could throw their shells only two-thirds of that distance. Harwood, however, intended to rely on teamwork to outwit and destroy the German commerce raider.

While patrolling the shipping lanes off the River Plate, a lookout spotted smoke to the north-east. Harwood had been right, and his ships were in exactly the right position to cope with the *Graf Spee*.

However, the *Graf Spee* had also spotted the British ships and made for them immediately. It was a fatal mistake. Langsdorff wanted a quick kill, but he would have done much better if he had kept out of range and hammered the British ships with his longer range guns. The British ships opened fire as their guns came within range, with *Exeter* being the first. Langsdorff's 11-inch guns hammered the *Exeter*, while his lighter armament engaged the British light cruisers. In accordance with the plan Harwood had worked out, the two British ships spread out, forcing the *Graf Spee* to fire in three directions at once. The *Exeter* retreated from the fight but then returned.

There are two conflicting rationales to account for what happened next. The first, which has been the conventional view of most historians, is that the *Graf Spee* was taking heavy punishment, as heavy as she had been dealing out, and Langsdorff was greatly hampered by knowing that he could not get repairs to his ship in the South Atlantic. He thought he might

Poster commemorating the first German air raid of World War II (16 October, 1939)

be able to destroy the British ships, but knew he would take so much damage that he could not continue his work, and might be unable to reach a friendly port.

He then tried to do what he should have done at the start. He tried to get out of range so that he could shoot without being hit back. However, it was too late. The British ships were too near and were as fast as the *Graf Spee*, although they were badly damaged.

After an hour and twenty minutes of receiving the punishing broadsides of her German opponent, the *Exeter* eventually had to give up. She limped away to the Falkland Islands to seek repairs. Harwood had to give up the fight. His own ship, the *Ajax*, had been badly damaged and half his guns put out of action. The *Achilles* was also badly damaged.

However, Langsdorff had also had enough. He knew that if there was a night action he might well be destroyed by the torpedoes of the two British ships and made up his mind to limp into Montevideo. However, it is possible that a minor head wound he had received during the action clouded his judgement, causing a temporary loss of nerve, and that this strongly influenced his judgement and what followed.

Langsdorff had hoped to be allowed to use the dry dock there to make repairs, but the government of Uruguay, no doubt under pressure from the British Embassy, insisted on applying the strict laws of neutrality. He could stay 24 hours and make repairs but he could not use the dockyard. If he overstayed his welcome, then his ship would be seized.

In the meantime, the British navy was rushing to the aid of Commodore Harwood. A carrier, a battle cruiser and several other ships, both cruisers and destroyers, were on their way. More importantly, the *Cumberland*, a battle cruiser, arrived from the Falkland Islands. She carried eight 8-inch guns, and with her arrival Harwood felt that any battle between himself and the *Graf Spee* would be a fair one, with a good chance of victory.

But Harwood was cheated of his victory. Langsdorff put most of his crew onto the safe refuge of a German merchant ship, and took out his ship but only far enough to scuttle her. He and his remaining crew escaped in lifeboats. Three days later Langsdorff, unable to bear the disgrace of losing his ship, and perhaps suffering from depression caused by his head wound, shot himself. It was the end of the most dangerous raider ship of all.

In fact, although some raiders did continue their work, the sinking of Raider 16 in November 1941 was effectively nearly the end of the raider war. (It is true that Raider 10, the *Thor*, set out on her second cruise in December 1941, and sank 56,000 tons of shipping, before she was destroyed by fire in Yokohama Bay in November 1942.) The British had now made it virtually impossible for raiders to operate in the Atlantic. Raider 45 (the *Komet*) was destroyed by British patrol vessels, and Raider 14 (the *Togo*) was forced to return to Germany following an air attack at Boulogne.

Another difficulty for the surface raiders was Hitler's own growing irritation with, and lack of faith in, the navy – apart, of course, from the U-boats, which continued to bring the battle to the enemy. After Raeder was replaced by Admiral Doenitz in 1942, the activities of the surface boats were restricted. Hitler was probably right – the Royal Navy was too much for him on the surface, and the time was fast approaching when the Allies proved too much for him on the land.

Appendix: The Stories of Tapscott and Widdicombe

Robert Tapscott

His parents were Cornish, and his father had served for a long time on a full-rigged sailing ship. However, in the end he became a pilot in Cardiff, which was a busy port during the heyday of the Welsh coal trade. Robert was born in Bristol in 1921, and never knew his father, who had either died or left home before he was old enough to take notice of the world. He was fond of soccer and was a good swimmer.

In 1936, he went to sea. As an apprentice, he received 6½ d. per day for his first year – which even at the time was a very low wage. He disliked the life, the dirty jobs an apprentice was given, and the generally bad conditions. In those days, the tramp steamer on which he worked carried extra coal on deck to save refuelling, all of which had to be moved below decks to the bunker.

In addition to these conditions, there was a limited supply of fresh meat and vegetables, and the bad food was itself in short supply. He worked four hours on and four off, on the normal watch system, and suffered from lack of sleep, as well as being casually bullied by the older men. After three voyages to the River Plate he quit, went farming for two months, and then decided to try the sea again as a mess-room boy on the *Grainton*, going to Cape Town for a cargo of cornmeal, and then to Rotterdam.

After that, Tapscott signed on to a ship called the *Nailsea Lass*, this time as an ordinary seaman, and carried supplies for the Republican side in the Spanish Civil War. (He was not politically engaged – his only motive seems to have been the 200 per cent bonus he received on his wages for running the risk.)

They delivered their cargo in Barcelona, and the crew managed to divert themselves ashore during the unloading process, watching the Catalan locals and meeting the Loyalist soldiers. They met some of the International Brigade, who seemed completely disillusioned with the whole process of the Civil War; so much so that two of them stowed away when the *Nailsea Lass* put to sea. There was a Canadian in the forecastle and a Londoner in the coal bunkers. After the captain found them, he was still suspicious there might be others, since he knew that several of the crew had palled up with the International Brigade while they were in port. He was right! A third man was found soon afterwards. The captain would have liked to have thrown them off the ship, but the third mate pleaded for them, and they were allowed to stay and journey back to England. However, when the ship reached England, the whole crew were paid off. The captain suspected that they had been pinching his beer, and sacked them all in order to get rid of the thieves.

Tapscott subsequently tried life on a passenger liner and cruised with the *Atlantis*, of the Royal Mail Line, whose schedule took them up to the Baltic, returning via the Kiel Canal. Many of the passengers took photographs but found that the Nazi guards seized their cameras and ripped out the films. When they docked, the crew were given four days' leave and returned to find that the *Atlantis* had been converted into a hospital ship. Tapscott was paid off. (He was then classified as an able-bodied seaman, which meant pay of £8.15s.0d per month, more than he had received as an ordinary seaman.) After that, he joined the *Orford* of the Orient Line, a ship of 20,000 tons, larger than his previous ships, and went out to the East to pick up 1,500 soldiers and cargo from Sydney, Australia. The troops were landed in Ismailia, Egypt, at the southern end of the Suez Canal.

The *Orford* then went on to Madagascar to collect 2,000 passengers to take back to Marseilles. On reaching Marseilles, the air raids were so heavy that the crew had to sleep ashore in air raid shelters. This was just as well, since one day they got up to find that their ship had been sunk by bombing. The crew had to travel to Cherbourg and back to England by ferry.

It was after this that Tapscott signed on to the *Anglo Saxon*. He had not intended to sail on her, having wished to sail on a ship with a couple of friends of his. However, the *Anglo Saxon*'s captain pressed him to join, being short of crew, and Tapscott agreed although with great misgivings. He did not say so, but this may have been a genuine premonition, and these misgivings stayed with him.

Roy Widdicombe

Roy Widdicombe was born in Totnes, Devon on 10 April 1910 – he was six feet tall and of dark, gypsy-like appearance. He was very different from Tapscott, being impetuous, stubborn and determined. His father had served in India as a soldier during the First World War. After that, he had opted for a quiet life, and went to Dartmouth, where he worked in the shipyards. His wife died when Roy was four years old, so the boy was brought up by his father's parents. It was not an altogether happy arrangement, for he disliked his grandmother.

Because he grew up in a seaside town, Widdicombe became familiar with boats and the sea. As a boy, he rowed and sailed dinghies, and even picked up small jobs, often playing truant from school. In spite of this, he won a scholarship to a grammar school. However, he opted for the *Conway*, a training ship for the merchant navy, and set off for that without any homesickness – perhaps because of his dislike for his grandmother. He was bad-tempered and quick with his fists, and probably knew that he could fit into any environment without fear of being bullied.

It is not known how he reacted to life aboard the *Conway*, which was moored on the Mersey, but it is probable that he enjoyed it, because it involved the kind of activities he found enjoyable. In the first year he studied knots, ropes, rigs, and simple navigation. The second and third years were taken up with sailing boats, more advanced navigation and the practical, everyday work on board the average merchant ship. He passed the Board of Trade examination and went to work as a deck boy. By the age of 15 he was classified as an able-bodied (AB) seaman, which was quite an achievement for somebody who was still so young. The *Conway* was the 'Eton and Oxford' of shipping life, and Widdicombe would have regarded himself as one of the élite of the sea.

He signed up on the Union Castle Line, and worked on the Cape Town run, and from there on he roamed all over the world, visiting Australia, the United States, South America, the Mediterranean and the West Indies. He preferred the hotter climates, and this influenced his choice of work.

He seems to have had some sense of humour. At one point he and three of his friends bought uniforms which looked like those worn by officers, and went ashore in them at Alexandria, no doubt hoping to succeed with the ladies by virtue of their dress. They got away with it without comment from authority, since there were no regulations preventing them from wearing what they liked off duty.

He must have applied himself to his work, because he eventually got a second mate's certificate. Now he had a uniform to wear as of right, and that certainly attracted the girls – five of them, including his future wife. He lived a colourful and varied life and his next ship was a tramp steamer, voyaging for Argentina, taking on beef from the canning factories at Rosario and Santa Fe. He sailed up the River Plate, negotiating the dangerous currents, and saw the half-wild gauchos who came to the river with cattle and hides to sell. He also visited the seamen's mission known as the 'Flying Angel', and enjoyed the usual seamen's entertainments.

Like Tapscott, he took advantage of the opportunities provided by the Spanish Civil War, working aboard the SS *Stanway*. There was money to earn, but also risks to run, as the *Stanway* found when she sailed to Bilbao. They ran into the start of a big offensive, and so sailed to Alicante where they found themselves at the receiving end of heavy bombing, with nothing to do but hang around the bars and get drunk. Although Tapscott and Widdicombe did not know each other then, they were both in Spanish ports. A bomb fell a few feet away from Widdicombe's ship. Tapscott was in Valencia, standing on the breakwater watching the shelling. They both certainly earned their extra 'hazard' bonus.

After this the *Stanway* returned to Antwerp and took on another cargo for Alicante. Widdicombe had an eye for a business opportunity and bought a load of American cigarettes for 2s. 6d a carton, and when the ship returned to Spain he bartered them for silk shirts, shawls, or anything else that was valuable, for cigarettes were scarce. Widdicombe actually obtained the suit in which he later got married through this trade.

When the Second World War started, Widdicombe had a foretaste of his later ordeal. His ship hit a mine and he found himself adrift in a lifeboat. However, this was not a great problem. There was plenty of food, blankets and rum on the boat, and they were rescued after only eight days. After this, he sailed to Baltimore again, but on his return found that Newport had been bombed. He wanted to stay with his wife and family after that, but decided to make one more voyage, signing up on the *Anglo Saxon* on 26 July 1940.

It was here that he met Tapscott, and they did not get on very well. Although they worked together as watchmates, it was just a matter of mutual toleration, and there was unseen friction, which surfaced more openly later. Widdicombe's temper is mentioned because it played a large part in the social problems between the occupants of the lifeboat after the *Anglo Saxon* sank. The details of the extraordinary incident of the sinking of the *Anglo Saxon* provide an example of the fate of those on the sharp end of raider operations.

The *Anglo Saxon* left home waters in Convoy OB 195 on 8 August 1940 (OB signifies 'outward bound'). Most of the ships (19) were from Liverpool, but the *Anglo Saxon* also joined them as part of a contingent of three ships from the Bristol Channel, apart from which there were five others from the Clyde.

The convoy left from Liverpool, sailing at an average of 5.7 knots, and went out into the Western Approaches. They had three escorts: two corvettes of the Flower Class, being *Periwinkle* and *Geranium*, and another, the *Vanoc*, a First World War V-Class destroyer built in 1917. She had been specially fitted out for escort duties in the second great conflict.

In mid-Atlantic, the convoy broke up, and all the ships went their separate ways. The *Anglo Saxon* headed for Argentina, where she was to take on a cargo of coal at Bahia Blanca. Her position at the time of the raider attack is not completely certain, but was probably west of the Cape Verde Islands.

The *Anglo Saxon* was built in 1929 by Short Bros of Sunderland and was owned by the Nitrate Producers Steamship Co., and managed by the Lawther Latta Company. Like all tramp steamers during the Second World War, she was painted grey. There was a crew of 40. Younger men predominated, and there were 15 men between 18 and 25 years old, 14 others between 25 and 40 and 11 between 41 and 56. There was also a boy of 16, one J. P. Takle. The chief engineer was E. Milburn. Among them there was a gunner, J. G. Penny, a 44-year-old ex-Royal Marine, who had signed on as a deck hand, although his duties were confined to the care and firing of the gun.

Tapscott and Widdicombe, who later turned out to be the only survivors, were put on the same watch with Gormley, an old Indian Army hand, who they both liked in spite of his rather tough character. The three of them made up an unofficial union committee to represent the seamen on any matters of work, watch rotas and (most importantly) food and the lack thereof. (Watches were organized in the usual way of the time – four hours on and four hours off.)

Widdicombe had a hot temper and the crew experienced a taste of this when one of them, a man called Elliott, said that their cook could not even boil water properly. Widdicombe had taught the cook his job regarding him as his protégé, and threatened to take Elliott up on deck and 'sort him out'. Elliott accepted the challenge but as he got up, Widdicombe punched Elliott in the face, cutting him with the heavy ring he wore. Tapscott felt Widdicombe had acted wrongly, and the incident added to the negative feelings between them. Thus matters stood at the time of the attack, which took place at night. It may be useful to look at where the crew were at the time.

Most of the off-duty crew were resting in the forecastles in the bows. Three firemen-trimmers and a greaser (engineer) had collected their 'black pan' evening meal and were eating it in their quarters. Three others were down in the stoke hole and one of the engineers was working in the engine-room. One of the three remaining firemen was playing cards with Tapscott in the sailors' forecastle, and all the other seamen were chatting or reading before going to sleep before they took the middle watch four hours later. The only other working crew member was Gormley, who was the lookout in the bows, and Widdicombe, who was actually steering the ship.

The third mate, fourth engineer, the catering ratings and Penny, the gunner, would have the cabins on the starboard side, and were probably in them at that time of night. The chief engineer, Milburn, would either be listening to the comments of the second engineer on engine performance in his cabin, or would be actually down in the engine-room seeing that everything was going well.

As for the senior officers, there are various accounts. One was that Captain Flynn was killed by machine gun bullets in his cabin, but Widdicombe says that he was killed by cannon fire when trying to dump the ship's documents. As for the second mate, he might have been sleeping in his bunk, but perhaps he was more likely to be drinking tea. There was an unofficial 'brew-up' tradition between the mate, radio operators, catering ratings and perhaps the gunner. They would take their mugs of tea and go to the steward's pantry or the galley and chat if they did not wish to go to their own rooms. The third mate was on watch on the bridge, and the fourth engineer was below with the greaser on duty.

(It is interesting to note that the ship lists a chief steward, R.N. Whitehorn, although he had failed to turn up. He actually joined the *Anglo Peruvian* and was sunk in that ship in February 1941.)

This was the *Anglo Saxon* and her crew at the time of the raider attack.

Tapscott's account of the attack

As he admitted he should have been up midships as he was 'stand-by' (spare-man) and therefore should be within call of the mate on watch, but he was engrossed in the game, the night was quiet, a mug of tea was at his elbow, he felt comfortable and had a winning hand. One of the ABs who had just come off watch started kidding him by remarking that the mate was shouting for him and was annoyed because he wasn't on stand by. Tapscott related that he got up to go on deck but the AB (Elliott) pulled him back and admitted he was pulling his leg.

Tapscott had barely retaken his seat when a shattering crash from the firemen's forecastle brought everyone to their feet. There were four more explosions almost simultaneously, shaking the length and breadth of the vessel. What was it? A mine or a torpedo? – they were stupefied by the suddenness of the detonations, but the fireman moved first, threw his cards down and shot up the companionway. The rest ran to their lockers and grabbed their life belts hurriedly strapping them on as they ran to the companionway. Tapscott was first after the fireman and as he reached deck level a blinding flash struck him with almost physical force. He knew he must follow the fireman's back and struggled to retain his balance as the ship shuddered beneath him. He was aware that behind him there was a mighty roar and a shocking blast – he felt himself fly forward, hit something hard and then he lost consciousness. What happened behind him, or to those following him he never knew. When he recovered his senses he saw he was on the starboard side of the deck about 20 feet from the companionway from where the blast had thrown him – he was flat on his face with his nose jammed up against the deck house. Momentarily he couldn't move – he felt no pain – nothing at all. He said he lay for what seemed a long time but it could only have been a few seconds, according to the general report.

The urge to live flowed back – he propped himself against the bulkhead and tried to move forward, reeling like a drunken man. He became aware of whizzing fiery streaks, some close to him, colliding with leaden thuds as they impacted on solid obstacles. He realized they were bullets – machine gun bullets with incendiaries, spraying over and on the ship. At first he could not think what was happening – it didn't occur to him the ship was being shelled.

A momentary cessation in firing gave him the chance to jump up and run midships towards the engineers' quarters – as he ran he knew he had been hurt but felt no pain, only numbness.

The firing recommenced, this time the incessant bang-bang of pom-pom guns demonstrating a more deadly assault. He crouched down as close to the deck as possible and was aware that someone was crouching beside him – he had no idea who it was.

The shooting raked the deck moving up for'ard, so he seized the chance to dive into the engineers' alleyway. Two men were coming out of the gloom, one carried a torch – but at this point the narration became confused, as it was obvious that the heavy shooting and shattering crescendo around him made it impossible to recall clearly the exact events happening in his vicinity. He dashed and scrambled until he was in the lee of the bridge structure, meanwhile incendiaries and bullets played across the deck. There was someone sheltering near the bridge, Penny the gunner. Recognition was almost instantaneous with the bursting of pom-pom shells nearby and Penny grunted as shrapnel went through his wrist. A few machine gun bullets sprayed near them in a steady hail and they both hit the deck together. Tapscott realized his head was on Penny's shoulder.

There was nothing they could do in that hail of shrapnel and bullets other than keep as low as possible. Tapscott remembered something moist and pulpy plastered his neck, and the deck beneath was slimy with what could have been blood. There was a constant and horrific din as metal smashed against metal – below them the hull of the ship reverberated with a chaotic clangour punctuated with detonating explosive shocks and crashes.

Penny was hit again by shrapnel, this time in the thigh, and long shuddering groans were forced from him. Later he told Tapscott he wished a bullet would finish him.

Tapscott knew that his own back was bleeding, fragments of the shell that blasted him across the deck had lodged there. His blood saturated his shirt but the slimy pool he was lying in was not his blood. He groped with his fingers outstretched and encountered the limp and torn body of a man. Afterwards he remembered thinking it might have been Paddy, if he had managed to dash from the for'ard head back to the bridge, hoping for safety. He was aware hearing feet trampling overhead and saw the dim shape of the jolly boat being lowered. When it drew level with the deck the lowering stopped and Penny hauled himself over the bulwark and rolled into it. Tapscott, half-jumped, half-dived into it and landed on top of the luckless gunner – at least they were in a lifeboat.

Widdicombe's account of the attack

Widdicombe was quite definite regarding the timing of the attack. He'd just glanced at the wheelhouse clock and noted it was 8.20 p.m. – that left him an hour and 40 minutes before the watch changed. It was then that the first salvo from the raider hit the *Anglo Saxon*'s poop deck, demolishing the gun and killing everyone on the forecastle. Explosions shook the ship – Widdicombe left the wheel and ran to the port side but there was nothing to be seen so he ran to the starboard side of the bridge and peered over the weather cloth. About a quarter of a mile away a dark shape was racing obliquely towards them – her guns firing as she came. He rushed back to the wheel and turned it hard to port.

A hail of lead and steel was pouring into the stern and moving for'ard. It cut through the *Anglo Saxon*'s upperworks with deadly effect and then, dropping to deck level, raked her fore and aft.

The 3rd mate whom Widdicombe had not been able to see ran in from the bridge shouting to Widdicombe to put the helm hard aport – he replied he had already done so. At this point the account is a little confused as to what precisely happened. The 3rd mate sheltered for a few seconds behind the concrete breastwork shielding the wheelhouse and the wireless cabin, meanwhile the noise of the sudden destructive attack made it difficult to hear or shout. Widdicombe recalled that that the 3rd mate told him he was going for orders and disappeared down the inside companionway – presumably going to the captain's cabin. That was the last time Widdicombe saw him. He continued to hold on to the wheel – the ship was blazing in numerous places, the noise deafened him and finally he left the wheel and ran on to the bridge again.

The raider was within 100 yards and could plainly be seen; he noted she was firing with every gun she had. Firing at a defenceless ship whose only gun they had already blown to pieces was 'no naval action'. A red glow lit up the *Anglo Saxon*'s poop, the starboard lifeboat was blazing whilst the jolly boat on that side was smashed to pieces.

Looking down, Widdicombe saw a body slumped against the bulwarks outside the captain's quarters – it was Captain Flynn. A machine gun burst had caught him full in the chest as he was dumping the ship's papers overboard. (This report differs from the mate's account written in the log). The 1st mate and the chief sparks scrambled up the port ladder on to the bridge. 'Antennas all shot away and sets smashed', Sparks reported to the mate, 'no hope of sending an S.O.S. now.'

The chief sparks huddled up against what was left of the concrete breastwork – he didn't appear to be afraid but unexpectedly invited Widdicombe to leave the bridge and go down with him for a drink. Widdicombe refused and remained at the wheel, but within a minute or so Sparks was back waving a bottle of rum from which he had taken a big swig. Again he beckoned Widdicombe to join him but the latter stayed where he was and the radio officer disappeared down the ladder and was never seen again. Widdicombe stated that it seemed an hour since the attack had started but glancing again at the clock he saw in fact that only six minutes had elapsed.

The mate came back on the bridge with the brief remark that the captain had gone and told Widdicombe to give him a hand to lower the jolly boat.

The ropes almost defied the mate's knife and Widdicombe stated he could hardly believe they were so tough and resistant. The lifeboat started to go down by the bow suddenly and fouled Widdicombe's hand, pulling it into the block where it jammed. The rope whipped Widdicombe's trousers down to the hips and seared his arm as it slashed by. Working frantically, Widdicombe managed to clear the block, the mate levelled the boat and they were able to lower it. As it passed down two men leaped into it from the weather deck – Tapscott and Penny.

At last they managed to lower the boat safely but there were other hazards to be reckoned with. Tapscott's job was to fend off the lifeboat from the ship's side, also to unhook the forward fall (the rope which allowed the jolly boat to be lowered down from the davits) so he clambered over the unfortunate gunner and cast off. The mate and Widdicombe slid rapidly down the lifelines into the boat and the 2nd sparks arrived at that moment and managed to follow them without a second to spare. Both the mate and Tapscott suffered burns and lacerations – the former when descending and the latter through trying to hold the boat alongside. No mention was made about Widdicombe's jammed hand. They were aware that the *Anglo Saxon*'s propeller, now half out of the water and still churning powerfully, and frighteningly drawing them nearer the stern area beneath the blazing poop. The easterly swell didn't help as it made matters even worse by driving them slowly towards the area from which they were trying to escape. The whirling blade only needed to touch the boat and they would be finished – in no time the blades would have slashed the men and the boat would have been destroyed.

Bibliography

Behrens, C. B. A. (1955) *Merchant Shipping and the Demands of War*, HMSO

Bekker, C. (1974) *The German Navy 1938-1945*, Hamlyn

Blair, C. (1997) *Hitler's U-Boat War*, Weidenfeld & Nicolson

Blake, G. (1946) *The Ben Line*, Thomas Nelson

Bradford, E. (1969) *The Mighty Hood*, Hodder and Stoughton [1977, Coronet]

Brenneke, H. J. (1954) *Ghost Cruiser HK33*, William Kimber & Co

Central Office of Information (1946) *The Battle of the Atlantic*, HMSO

Churchill, W. S. (1950) *The Second World War*, Vols I-VI, Cassell

Cubbin, G. (2003) *Harrisons of Liverpool*, The World Ship Society – Ships in Focus Publications

Detmers, T. (1959) *The Raider Kormoran*, William Kimber & Co [1975, Tandem]

Dove, P. (1956) *I Was Graf Spee's Prisoner*, Viking Press

Frischauer, Wills & Jackson, Robert (1955) *The Navy's Here: The Altmark Affair*, Victor Gollancz

Gibson, C. (1987) *Death of a Phantom Raider*, Robert Hale

Haldane, R. A. (1978) *The Hidden War*, Robert Hale

Hardy, W. M. (1960) *Wolfpack*, Hamish Hamilton [1964, Four Square]

HMSO (1942) *Ark Royal*

HMSO (1984) *British Vessels Lost at Sea 1939-45*, Patrick Stephens

Hough, R. (1986) *The Longest Battle*, Weidenfeld & Nicolson

Hoyt, E. P. (1970) *Raider 16*, Lancer Books

Jones, G. P. (1941) Two Survived, 'The Reader's Digest', Vol 39, no. 234 (October 1941)

Lund, A. (1993) *The Raider and the Tramp*, Alfred Lund – Maxprint Colour Printers

Melville, C. (1990) *Luftwaffe over the East Coast of Scotland*

Middlebrook, M. (1976) *Convoy*, Allen Lane [1978, Penguin]

Muggenthaler, A. K. (1977) *German Raiders of World War II*, Prentice-Hall

Paine, L. (1998) *Ships of the World*, Conway Maritime Press

Poolman, K. (1956) *Ark Royal*, William Kimber & Co [1974, New English Library]

Poolman, K. (1981) *Periscope Depth*, William Kimber & Co

Poolman, K. (1985) *Armed Merchant Cruisers*, Martin Secker & Warburgh Ltd.

Pope, D. (1956) *The Battle of the River Plate*, William Kimber & Co [1999, Chatham Publishing]

Ramsey W. G., editor (1987) *The Blitz Then and Now*, vol. 1, Battle of Britain Prints International

Schmalenbach, P. (1979) *German Raiders*, Naval Institute Press

Shirer, W. L. (1959) *The Rise and Fall of the Third Reich*, Secker & Warburg [1984, Book Club Associates]

Terraine, J. (1989) *Business in Great Waters*, Leo Cooper

Townsend, P. (1970) *Duel of Eagles*, Simon & Schuster

Van der Vat, D. (1988) *The Atlantic Campaign*, Hodder and Stoughton

Walmsley, L. (1941), *Fisherman at War*, Collins

Williams, A. (2002) *The Battle of the Atlantic*, BBC Worldwide

Woodward, D. (1955) *The Secret Raiders*, William Kimber & Co

Periodicals

Edinburgh Evening News
Hull Daily Mail
Illustrated History of World War II
Liverpool Daily Post and Echo
Newcastle Chronicle and Journal
Scarborough Evening News
Scotsman Publications
Sea Breezes
Sunday Mail Magazine
War Illustrated
War Weekly
Whitby Gazette
World War Investigator
World War II Review

Archives and Institutions

602 Fighter Squadron (City of Glasgow)
603 Fighter Squadron (City of Edinburgh)
Imperial War Museum
Lloyds, Shipping Losses World War II
Public Record Office

That Curious Fellow, Captain Basil Hall, RN

James McCarthy

- A fascinating account of his extraordinary life and times
- Record of naval history in the first half of the 19th century
- An indefatigable traveller whose early descriptions of Korea, China and Borneo and naval life made him famous
- An insight into Edinburgh and London high society from previously unpublished and revealing correspondence

Son of a scientifically-minded Scottish aristocrat, Basil Hall joined the Royal Navy at the age of 13 in 1802. His first naval engagements in America and Spain during the Peninsular War are described, as are his travels in India and the Far East. His renowned interview with Napoleon, while still a prisoner on St. Helena is featured. He was a confidante of Sir Walter Scott, Dickens and many other distinguished authors of his day.

Renowned for his curiosity and energy, he became a popular writer himself based on his world-wide travels and adventures, including his involvement in the liberation of Peru and friendship with General San Martin. He embarked on an epic, 10,000-mile journey with his family in North America and twice journeyed across the sub-continent of India under the patronage of Admiral Sir Samuel Hood, providing delightful vignettes of Indian life of the time. Subsequent travels in Europe introduce personalities such as Lord Byron and the eccentric Countess Purgstall.

Although the narrative of his journey in the United States earned him great opprobrium from Americans for his conservative attitudes, his support in Edinburgh to the great American bird painter, John James Audubon, was greatly appreciated by the artist.

As an amateur scientist, Hall made important contributions to nautical astronomy, geology and naval technology, being a Fellow of both the Royal Society and the Royal Society of Edinburgh. Among his scientific friends were Sir John Herschel, Mary Somerville, and Sir Humphrey Davy, among many others.

He was in the unusually privileged position of moving among the upper echelons of British society's distinguished writers, scientists and politician, thus providing a fascinating insight into the mores and manners of high society in Edinburgh and London. The inclusion of previously unpublished and often revealing correspondence has contributed to the first full biography of a very colourful individual and his times.

Readership: This fascinating book will be of immense appeal to everyone with an interest in naval history, exploration, travel, scientific discoveries and historical biographies.

ISBN 978-184995-033-6   240 × 170mm   208pp   52 b/w illustrations   softback   £18.99

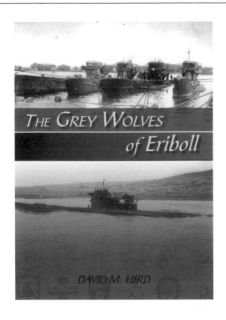

The Grey Wolves of Eriboll

David M. Hird

- The first detailed investigation which reveals Loch Eriboll's pivotal role in the surrender of German U-boats to northern Scotland in May, 1945

- Enriched with personal recollections of combatants and also by defeated crew members

- Liberally illustrated with contemporary photographs and maps

The surrender of the German U-boat fleet at the end of World War II was perhaps the principal event in the war's endgame which signified to the British people that peace really had arrived. It is little known that the majority of the surrenders of U-boats on active west-European sea patrols in May 1945 were supervised in Loch Eriboll, an isolated sea loch on Scotland's far north-westernmost coast.

Loch Eriboll's attraction as the reception port was its isolation and its safe, deep-water anchorage ideal for the arrival of armed U-boats that might still be intent on one last show of defiance. News of the momentous event was heavily censored; nothing appeared in the local press. Thirty-three U-boats, their officers and men surrendered between 10th and 22nd May 1945.

The pivotal role played by Loch Eriboll in ending the U-boat menace is little-known and lesser celebrated – this book rights that wrong.

From the reviews:

'The author has assembled a fascinating amount of 'personal recollections' from both German and Allied people, he looks at the naval escorts involved - 21st Escort Group and the 9th Canadian Escort Group and details every U-boat that visited Loch Eriboll. Most fascinating is the author's selection of 'contemporary information' in the form of extracts from how *The Scotsman* newspaper saw it. An excellent book covering a significant naval event in the immediate days following the ending of combat against Nazi Germany'. *Warships*

'...well researched book... ...this fascinating book describes how the surrender of the U boat fleet was put in place...' *Ships Monthly* – **Book of the Month**

'...well researched, fact filled and eminently readable account of this mass surrender... David Hird's excellent book highlights a little known period at the end of the war when the "Grey Wolves" were temporary visitors. It comes highly recommended.' *The Northern Times*

ISBN 978-1904445-32-6   240 × 170mm   160pp   liberally illustrated with b/w photos and maps   £16.99

Island Base
Ascension Island in the Falklands War
Captain Bob McQueen

Captain Bob McQueen was Senior Officer, Ascension Island during the Falklands War and *Island Base* is the previously untold story of how Ascension Island was crucial to the success of British operations during the conflict.

From the Foreword by Admiral Sir Alan West, First Sea Lord
'Much has been written about the war, but very little about the island base... This book explains how the island was an essential stepping stone in the execution of a daring plan … Lack of facilities required much improvisation... which was accomplished with commendable dedication and good humour by our armed forces'.

From the reviews:

'...*Island Base* is an important aspect of the history of a war... Excellent photographs provide an intriguing record of all aspects of Ascension... since no journalists were allowed … The book gives a fascinating view of the heady atmosphere of "going to war" and an authoritative overview of the logistics involved...' *The Northern Mariner*

'...Would appeal to anyone who served on Ascension as it brings back vivid memories. ...Recommended'. *Air Mail*

'...An authoritative and enjoyable account of life on Ascension Island throughout the campaign. ...With an easy-going style and dry humour, Capt. McQueen gives lively descriptions of constantly hectic life... First-hand accounts from others involved … all lend ample colour and give differing perceptions of the logistical miracles performed daily. The photographs... do help complete this engaging spotlight on Ascension...' *Airforces Monthly*

'...An important contribution to the history of Operation Corporate … and there is no excuse for anyone with an interest at any level in the Falklands conflict not having it on their bookshelf'. *Navy News*

ISBN 978-1904445-18-0   240 x 170mm   144pp   liberally illustrated inc. colour section   softback   £16.99